The Elements of Editing

THE ELEMENTS

A Modern Guide for

OF EDITING

Editors and Journalists

by Arthur Plotnik

COLLIER BOOKS
MACMILLAN PUBLISHING COMPANY
NEW YORK

COLLIER MACMILLAN PUBLISHERS
LONDON

Macmillan Publishing Company
866 Third Avenue, New York N.Y. 10022
Collier Macmillan Canada, Inc.

Library of Congress Cataloging in Publication Data
Plotnik, Arthur.
The elements of editing.
Includes bibliographies and index.
1. Editing 2. Journalism—Editing. I. Title.
PN162.P55   1984   070.4'1   83-18759

ISBN 0-02-047430-X

First Paperback Edition 1984

10 9 8 7 6

Macmillan books are available at special discounts for bulk purchases for sales promotion, premiums, fund-raising, or educational use. For details, contact:
Special Sales Director
Macmillan Publishing Company
866 Third Avenue
New York, N.Y. 10022

The Elements of Editing is also published in a hardcover edition by Macmillan Publishing Company.

Printed in the United States of America

Two things are required from every specialized treatise: it should clarify its subject and, in the second place, but actually more important, it should tell us how and by what methods we can attain it and make it ours.

Longinus (ca. 213-273),
On the Sublime

Two things are required from every specialized treatise: it should clarify its subject and, in the second place, but actually more important, it should tell us how and by what methods we can attain it and make it ours.

Longinus (ca. 213–273),
On the Sublime

Contents

Preface:
Grope No More in Vain

I HAVE WRITTEN THIS SMALL BOOK because a thousand times
in my career I have groped for it and come up empty-handed.
Weighty editorial texts and manuals are everywhere; but for
editors in search of handy, practical, wide-ranging, and short-
winded advice, books have not provided the answer. In fact,
never was my quest for such advice more frustrating than at the
Library of Congress, where, as a staff editor, I was privy to the
full collection of some fifty-five million volumes.

Then, as an editorial novice, I needed a little book of advice.
Later, as an editorial supervisor, I longed for a good primer I
could use in training new staff. Instead, I found myself repeat-
ing the same basic elements to one trainee after another—
mainly the elements I had acquired tediously or traumatically as
a student editor, freelance writer, newspaper reporter, and editorial intern.

Still unsure of my own expertise, I hesitated to gather these
elements into a manual. But during the next dozen years as

assistant, associate, and chief editor of various publications, I
kept notes on the training needs of new staff and on the best
advice I was able to pass along. This book is an expansion of
those notes and a distillation of contemporary practice in editing. It is based on two principles: (1) that most on-the-job
editorial training focuses on the employer's unique requirements and not on general editorial basics, and (2) that most
textbooks, for all their mass, do not address the range of
practical problems a new editor will confront in the course of a
year.

Another hard truth is that most editorial executives would
rather proofread five-point type than train new staff in the
mundane elements of editing. This book will lighten the basic-
training load of busy editors or at least mitigate their guilt over
doing nothing.

An editor can always hand new staff the house style manual
and refer them to scores of texts and night extension courses.
But these tactics will turn off even the most ambitious learners.
They have not come to exhaust themselves by wading through
tomes of knowledge or massive compendiums of editorial data.
They want what I had always wanted—enough guidance to let
them get on with the work and learn by doing.

The Compleat Editor

Must an editor be well-rounded? Yes. On a small publication,
the nature of editorial work is eclectic, to say the least. And in a
large operation, no editor is an island; any staffer's ignorance of
problems outside a single specialty diminishes the final product
over the long run.

Well-roundedness increases one's mobility—laterally, from
specialty to specialty, as well as upward toward management.
An entire staff of well-rounded editors is a coherent staff; its
members understand one another's roles and are flexible
enough to operate under even the most crippling circumstances, which are so common in the communications business.

If our colleges and journalism schools produced well-rounded beginners, perhaps this book would be unnecessary. We already know that many general graduates, though film- and computer-literate, cannot edit their own résumés. But what about the journalism school graduates?

In a 1978 study* based on survey returns from eighty-four magazine editors, a professor of communications came up with this finding: "Indeed, 57% . . . agreed that journalism graduates are poorly prepared or not prepared at all to handle magazine editorial positions, and that opinion was shared by editors of small and large publications alike."

My little volume of editorial advice can in no way make up for an inadequate educational background. But somewhere between that compleat education and the few basic instructions editors may shout at newcomers between deadlines, I felt there was a place for a compact, friendly training package. I have already used this package, in unpublished form, with encouraging success. Now when you and I grope for the book, it will be there.

*Edwin O. Haroldsen and Kenneth E. Harvey. "Frown Greets New J-Grads in Magazine Job Market." *Journalism Educator*, July 1979.

Acknowledgments

IN ADDITION TO THOSE I HAVE CITED in the text for their assistance, I thank the following people for their kind and expert advice: Martha J. Hamilton, Helen Wright, William Miller, Joel Lee (Chapter 6), Billy Collins (Chapter 8), John Tripp (Chapter 9), and Amanda Parsons (Chapter 10).

The Elements of Editing

The Editorial Personality
GOOD AND BAD COMPULSIVENESS

WHAT KIND OF PERSON makes a good editor? When hiring new staff, I look for such useful attributes as genius, charisma, adaptability, and disdain for high wages. I also look for signs of a neurotic trait called compulsiveness, which in one form is indispensable to editors, and in another, disabling.

A magazine editor I worked with in the last days of linotype was compulsive about finding broken *p*'s in galley proofs. He was an excellent and humane person, a Londoner with a background in fine-edition publishing; but his experience hadn't prepared him for the demands of a national trade monthly. Had his compulsiveness been the kind that functions positively for editors, he would have directed it at getting the raw material *in* and the magazine *out*. Instead, while deadlines burned, he fiddled with galleys, searching for *p*'s with amputated descenders.

"You see," he explained, as a prelude to cursing out the

linotype operators, "if the lead is heated insufficiently, it will fail to trickle into the base of the *p* matrix."

The linotype operators had a word or two for such obsessive behavior; but for our own purposes we may call it dysfunctional or editor-related compulsiveness.

An editor edits above all to communicate to readers, and least of all to address the sensibilities of editorial colleagues. Functional or reader-related compulsiveness is the neurotic drive enabling editors to do a full six weeks of work in a four-week cycle, month after month. It is the built-in alarm, the time-bomb system that glows red when there are omissions, delays, and errors which, if not corrected, will devastate deadlines and subvert communication. In the editorial context, this type of compulsiveness is appropriate and manifests itself in several areas. But self-serving, retentive, fastidious, fetishistic, and even some aesthetic and ethical types of compulsiveness have no place in mass communications under deadlines; they must be purged from new staff members for the sake of the staff's longevity in the field.

The distinctions are best explained by example. Below are a few manifestations of dysfunctional and functional compulsiveness that I have seen among editorial staff. Note them well, because more than likely your boss will come to judge you by them.

Signs of Dysfunctional
(Editor-Related) Compulsiveness

Holding to favorite rules of usage,
whatever the effect on communication.

Some compulsives will work through a manuscript, and even galleys, changing every "till" to "until" or vice versa, depending on the grammatical ear they brought with them to the job and have never tuned to the demands of deadlines. Chief editors are usually the least flexible, stamping out perfectly acceptable words and phrases with great ceremony or waving their favorite (and usually outdated) usage handbooks. Although it is appropriate for editors to rail against the depreciation of English into jargon and colloquial swill, they must stop short of a self-styled purism and allow for some variety of expression. When chief editors wave Fowler, John Simon, and other guardians of the trust, staff should wave back *Miss Thistlebottom's Hobgoblins*, Theodore Bernstein's debunking of sacred cows in usage, or William and Mary Morris's *Harper Dictionary of Contemporary Usage*, which allows for differences of "expert" opinion.

Musing for fifteen minutes on whether to use a hairline or one-point rule.

This type of quandary results from a compulsion toward "consistency," usually for its own sake and not to aid the reader. I have seen too many editors search through piles of back issues to determine "how we have done it in the past." Did we use a hairline or one-point rule to separate the caption from the main text? I tell my editors to be consistent within the *present* issue and, when we have the time, we will work up a style rule based on good sense—not precedent.

A similar compulsive symptom is resetting a page of footnotes because a comma has been used after place of publication (e.g., New York, Doubleday, 1981) instead of the colon sometimes preferred. If the typesetting is done and the footnotes are consistent within the article, *live* with it. Spend the time you have saved by checking the spelling of unusual author names—much more important from the reader's point of view.

Changing every passive construction to an active one.

A little Strunk and White is a dangerous thing. Some editors are driven by a cursory reading of *The Elements of Style* to change such sentences as "the outcry was heard round the world" to "everyone in the world heard the outcry." True, the active voice is generally more forceful, and a procession of passive constructions is a safe cure for insomnia. But the passive voice is a perfectly legitimate alternative when used for variety or to emphasize a key word in the sentence by making it the subject (e.g., "outcry" in the example above).

Concentrating on negative rather than positive space in layout.

The negative, or white space, on a page of print is an important design element, but unworthy of compulsiveness. I know one editor who would delete a prize photo of a trapped miner so as not to trap white space in a photo layout. More common are the editors who will not place a subhead where it is needed in the text because the space opened up would touch a break in an adjacent column, creating a forbidden "tombstone" of white space. The solution that considers deadlines and readers is not to remake the page; it is to put in the subhead and hope other columns will break better.

Some editors argue that white space *is* reader-oriented, for its careful use is soothing to the eye and helps present the positive elements—the type and art. Its misuse, they argue, can be jarring and confusing. All true; but deadlines force compromise, trade-offs, and priorities, with no room for the retentive-compulsive approach.

Among other compulsive acts in this category are holding up pages because the folios (page numbers) are a quarter pica ($\frac{1}{24}$ inch) too high, or because one double *f* was set *ff* instead of with the preferable ligature *ff*, or because all the *n*'s were an eyelash off alignment. Infinite attention to such details would be ideal were it not that the energy spent on them is almost always stolen from the more important and challenging tasks of the editor—for example, finding good material, making it communicate, and getting it out when it is timely.

Signs of Functional (Reader-Oriented) Compulsiveness

Following up.

Editors who love their readers may also cherish their authors, coeditors, and production people; but readers are the only group entitled not to be told the same thing twice, three times, and more. A polite name for hounding people is "nudging," and systematic nudging is called "following up." It is a compulsive trait of effective editors, for in the harried, whacky world of communications, virtually *nothing happens when it is supposed to happen without well-timed reminders*.

Authors and artists do not meet deadlines or deliver all requested materials. Advertising agencies fail to meet closing dates. Production people lose sight of editorial priorities. Printers and circulation departments forget special instructions.

The mechanics of follow-up could not be simpler. As part of carrying out an assignment, an editor schedules the necessary follow-ups on a day-by-day calendar. If the editor is to be out of the office for a day or more, the calendar is checked in advance and the follow-ups rescheduled or delegated.

Follow-up diplomacy is more difficult. A thin line separates the "necessary" from the superfluous and irritating. As a rule of thumb, the longer the lead time, the more follow-ups need to be programmed. Too much follow-up, however, can degenerate into white noise, or the editor may be written off as a too-frequent crier of "Wolf!" But most new editors, not wanting to be pests, err on the side of too little follow-up. They give an author a deadline and wait in good faith until the day after it falls before making a call. They notify a busy printer by phone that a lighter paper stock should be acquired for next year's volume, trusting that the printer will take it from there.

Trust and good faith. The words mean something different in

communications than in the rest of life. Editors show trust and good faith by signing and renewing contracts, not by expecting people to have infallible memories and priorities identical to their own.

New editors who understand this principle will soon develop into functionally compulsive pests. They needn't be insufferable. After all, "routine follow-up" is generally accepted as good business practice, and a reminder can always be tactful. Editors must also learn to distinguish between those who need frequent or infrequent nudging, firm or soft nudging. They must learn the best timing for a nudge.

Before these refinements are mastered, however, novitiates must recite Plotnik's mantra of follow-up until it becomes instinctive and obsessive:

NOTHING HAPPENS WHEN IT IS SUPPOSED TO HAPPEN WITHOUT WELL-TIMED REMINDERS

Rewriting every headline that fails to motivate readership.

Editors who simply cannot let an ineffective headline see print may drive staff bananas, but there is method to their madness: The best story in the world is worthless if no one reads it. Media with staff who specialize in head writing are fortunate. Some publications—such as a tabloid out of Florida—will pay a headline writer obscene sums of money because they know how heads affect readership. But in small editorial operations, almost every staffer has a shot at writing heads and must internalize two basic rules or live with rewrites. A headline must:

1. Let the reader know how the story differs from previous stories on similar topics; and
2. Pique the reader's interest anew.

WEST SIDE FIRE KILLS FIVE piques only a sense of déjà vu. FIVE DIE AS SMOKE DETECTOR FAILS does the job if the smoke-detector angle is new. If not, the writer must dig deeper into the particulars or reach for some device to stir interest.

"FOOLPROOF" INSULATOR MELTS; FIVE DIE IN FLAMES, or "BARGAIN" SMOKE DETECTOR BLAMED IN DEATH OF FIVE, and so on. The challenge to write fresh headlines is perhaps greatest on trade publications, covering the same narrow subject in issue after issue. Challenges, however, are what editors say they want.

Quadruple-checking of page proofs.

Murphy's Law assures us that no amount of proofreading will uncover all the errors of a work about to be published. The questions are, how many re-readings are reasonable and when should compulsiveness be applied? In my experience I have found that two editorial-level readings of galleys and two of pages will catch 99 percent of the errors. Unfortunately, the remaining one percent are so often the mistakes that cause not just embarrassment, but trouble—for example, erroneous numbers for ordering merchandise or securing additional information, misspelled names in bibliographies, and transposed identifications under portraits. The editor who understands how people feel about such errors will compulsively check for them in third and fourth readings of page proofs. The extra effort rarely pays off and may appear neurotic; but it is healthy from the point of view of the reader, who depends on the editor's accuracy.

Staring at type specifications a full ten seconds.

A type specification is a coded instruction indicating the family and size of type and the width and depth of lines. It is directed at the typesetter* and might look like this: Set 8/10 HM ital × 13½ pi, fl. l., rag. rt. (Translation: Set this section of manuscript copy in 8-point Helvetica medium italic type on 10 points of vertical space per line; the lines are flush against the

---

*Or to the typesetting function of an in-house VDT (video display terminal) system. Resetting by computer may be faster and less costly than by the old procedures, but it is still to be avoided.

left margin and roughly aligned on the right, no more than 13½ picas wide.)

A simple typesetting code can carry instructions like a string of DNA, and the instructions are crucial. Once the specs have been determined, they must be indicated with brutal clarity on the manuscript, then checked and (compulsively) rechecked before the manuscript leaves for the typesetting operation. I have seen thousands of lines require expensive resetting because the specs are assumed to have been correctly marked the first time. Suppose a harried editor had written "HB ital" instead of "HM ital" in the specs above, and no one had checked it. Back would come the type in Helvetica *boldface* italic, each dark letter like a boot in the horrified editor's face. The manuscript so marked would have to be reset, probably late in the cycle, when time as well as money is running short.

A second editor, whether higher or lower in the hierarchy, must stare at least ten seconds at every type spec and ask this question: Is there anything unusual about the specs and, if so, was it intended? Ordinarily, typesetters will not scrutinize the editor's specs, nor will a computer, unless painstakingly programmed to do so. Trade practice bids typesetters to "follow the manuscript (including specs) even if it flies out the window." So as not to fly out with it in despair, editors need only to incorporate the ten-second rule in their own standard practice.

The compulsive editor, when checking the specs on an article, can't help checking also for such items as initial capital and closing dingbat, if they are used routinely. These decorative items have a way of being forgotten by the first editor of the manuscript—unless that editor, too, is functionally compulsive and puts them in immediately.

Reading every word in its final context.

This act does not necessarily indicate mistrust of the manuscript editors, typesetters, proofreaders, layout editors, keyliners, and photoengravers—although most chief editors mistrust them all. It is more an act comparable to checking gas-stove burners one last time before leaving home on vacation. Because the whole is greater than the sum of its parts, it must be reviewed as a whole. And indeed such a review may turn up the most atrocious errors: two enormous headings transposed on related stories; a pair of arch-enemy advertisers on facing pages; the middle third of the lead article missing entirely. These are the editorial black holes that may go undetected under the proofreader's microscope, and one ounce of compulsiveness can avert a cosmic disaster.

> *As soon as one issue is put to bed,*
> *insisting that work begin on the next.*

Here the editor is no more compulsive than the ant who prepared for winter while the grasshopper made merry. It is bad enough having to do six weeks' work in a four-week cycle. Slacking off for a week and trying to make up for it in the remaining three only increases the pressure, panic, ill will, errors, and compromises in quality at the end of the cycle. The most human tendency is to launch a four-day pencil-sharpening project after an issue goes to bed. It is an editorial administrator's duty to keep the pressure on—within reason—and the production flowing throughout the cycle. Such is the heat of the editorial kitchen, and the staffer who can't take it belongs elsewhere. The best staff editors quickly develop this compulsion on their own and need not be whipped to get cracking.

Balancing Compulsions

Most editorial staffs seem to have a "house compulsive" whom the others regard as the air traffic controller of their artistic flights. Serious new staffers, rather than relying on other compulsives, tailor their own obsessive responses to the needs and desires of their audience. If the audience wants daily news, the editor is compulsive about speed; if the audience wants weekly reports, accuracy is the prime factor; if the audience favors form over content, then aesthetic compulsiveness may be appropriate. Editors of a definitive dictionary cannot be too fastidious; copy-desk editors of all-news radio have opposite priorities.

New staffers may find the compulsions necessary on the job to be in conflict with their natural drives. Tics will result. Work them out on weekends; but during the week, communication to a particular audience is one's reason for being—and for being functionally nuts.

2

Order Out of Chaos

TEN BASIC STEPS IN "PROCESSING" A MANUSCRIPT

WHEN TOLD TO "EDIT" A MANUSCRIPT, no two editors in the world will go about it in the same way. The act of editing means many things to many people; it is seen as an art, a craft, a catharsis, a crusade. Editing becomes all these and more eventually, but to professional editors it is first a job that results in a product. Editors are paid to "process" words into communication "packages."

The terms may seem crass. Is editing like processing fat into soap or packaging toilet tissue? Yes and no. Some editorial products do call to mind these commodities. But here the words *process* and *package* mean only that manuscripts undergo "a particular method, system, or technique of preparation, handling, or other treatment designed to effect a particular result," and that the results are most effective when "organized into or constituting a compact unit."*

Webster's Third New International Dictionary of the English Language, Unabridged.

Although no one method of handling and preparing a manuscript prevails throughout the communications industry, certain basic steps do underlie the operating procedures of most editorial offices. A brief and friendly guide to these basics is usually unavailable to new staffers, who are assumed to have prior training in—or a feel for—general handling and treatment of manuscripts. Some do. Those who don't may find a few clues in the house style book, but several of the most crucial elements in the editorial process will remain a mystery.

Using the magazine environment as an example, I have identified ten basic steps of manuscript processing and offered some nuts-and-bolts advice to go along with them. The steps are designed as a mechanical framework within which an editor will develop creative, individualistic approaches. Although their sequence will vary somewhat from one operation to another, they represent what editorial staff do on most publications to fully "edit" a manuscript.

The Steps

1. *Acquisition.* Securing a manuscript may be the most stimulating of all editorial activities or the most tedious; it is usually something in between. It can mean wheeling and dealing with agents over *perdreaux truffés* or a seaside dialogue with a literary recluse. It can mean being handed the boss's banquet speech. More likely, a manuscript will be acquired or "developed" after prolonged communication with a moderately accomplished individual who happens to have something timely to say.

A manuscript may spring from almost any source: a chance meeting at a conference, a rousing speech overheard there, an author's query in the mail. Often the editors take the initiative, triggered by any number of stimuli; they see a good piece of writing in another publication; they read of a heroic or infamous act worthy of more attention; or, in a brainstorm, they simply connect a hot idea with a likely author.

A few manuscripts are still drawn from the slush pile of unsolicited materials. Most editors, reluctant to stifle the dreams of would-be contributors or their own dreams of discovering new talent, devote much time to handling, reading, and returning many thousands of words that will never see print. One of the most common activities of editors, in fact, is saying no. The business of rejection is exhausting, sometimes painful, and leaves nothing to show for the effort. Yet someone with editorial judgment has to do it.

My advice in the matter of rejection is not to give advice to the rejected—with one exception: If you are suggesting a revision for resubmission, be generous and specific in your advice and carefully noncommittal. Otherwise, simply express your regret that the rejected manuscript "was not among our selections for forthcoming issues." Further advice, however much it was sought and however kind your intentions, usually ends up being resented. If you want to teach writing or play agent, do it on the side. If you want to edit, don't exhaust your energy and imagination in the rejection process.

For solicited manuscripts, a relatively sober letter must always back up the freewheeling negotiations with the prospective contributor. The letter spells out your interests in fine detail, both to guide the author and, should a brawl develop later, to protect you against damages. Within the letter, editors should boldly and abundantly reveal the concepts they have in mind; but they must also encourage the author to be inventive. The acquisition letter suggests some of the terms that might be included in a formal agreement. It provides a deadline date and the preferred length, with maximum. Along with the letter may go a copy of the publication's general guidelines for authors, if not otherwise provided.

The acquisition letter is not a contract. Ideally the editor remains noncommittal at this stage, asking to see manuscripts on "speculation" only. Accepting materials by prior agreement and not on their own merits inhibits the editor's quality control and ultimately cheats the readers.

The trouble is that not every author wants to slave away at research, take risks, spend money, and pound out two or three drafts of a custom-tailored article on the speculation that it might meet your editorial criteria—not for the few hundred dollars paid by most magazines, and not for the "token of appreciation," "honorarium," or "prestige" that nonprofit publications offer. The better the writers and the lengthier the projects, the more essential it becomes to guarantee publication and payment. Some authors will demand at least a sizeable "kill" fee should their work not be used.

Authors have every right to demand such guarantees and even advance payments; editors have every right to deny them. I would advise both parties to go for whatever they can get; the conflict will be resolved quickly enough by the laws of supply and demand—the question of who needs whom more. "Name" authors rarely have to write on speculation; unknowns frequently do. For those in between, some sort of kill fee may have to be worked out, or perhaps a half-commitment: "Although we cannot accept manuscripts sight unseen, we are confident your work will measure up to our criteria for publication. We encourage you to proceed."

The terms used in acquisition activities may sometimes confuse the newcomer. An article may be "solicited" through either an informal, nonbinding expression of interest or an outright offer of compensation. An article is "assigned" or "commissioned," however, only by a formal agreement whose terms are binding on both parties. In copyright parlance (see below), the latter two terms may translate into contracting "work for hire," as opposed to leasing or purchasing a completed work as literary property.

Editors who work regularly with certain reliable freelance authors will usually offer them an assignment or commission to write on a particular topic for a set fee and surrender of proprietary rights. Some writers would surrender life and limb for guaranteed payment; but it is worth remembering that a manuscript written on speculation may be sold to any party at any price and on whatever terms the author can negotiate.

2. *Agreement.* When the editor has outlined the requirements of a "work for hire" or when a manuscript written on speculation suits the editor's needs, the publisher and the writer (or agent or proprietor) sign a formal agreement. An editor often signs as a representative of the publisher.

The agreement may be in the form of a standard printed contract, setting forth terms the publisher offers most authors. It may be a standard contract with a few additions and modifications, or a custom-made contract. Whatever the form, it must describe the rights being acquired and the compensation, if any, being given for them.

Which rights should be acquired? Basically, there are two categories of rights to nondramatic literary works: rights to use and rights to own.

Use by licensing

For the right to use a work, the publisher acquires from its owner a "license" for explicit purposes. The license may permit, say, use of an article in the publisher's magazine and reproduction of the article in publisher-authorized microform editions of that magazine. The publisher may want to secure also the right to include the article in anthologies drawn from the magazine—and may have to pay extra to get it. In small newspapers and magazines, these three rights—initial use, microform reproduction, and inclusion in anthologies—are probably the three most common of those acquired by license. The licensing agreement need be no more than a paragraph. The more ambitious the publisher and the hotter the property, of course, the more complicated the agreement. The contracts thicken with sections on future and subsidiary rights ranging from translation to television. Whatever the terms under licensing, however, the publisher is only a restricted user and not the owner of the literary property.

Ownership by copyright

A publisher may want to become the owner of a property that has promise of future value. Ownership is not always preferable to licensing and not always more profitable, but when it seems worthwhile, the publisher will seek to acquire exclusive proprietary rights—i.e., copyright.

An editor's introduction to copyright constitutes a later chapter. For now, copyright is mentioned only as part of the "agreement" step in processing a manuscript.

Instead of an agreement offering compensation for certain limited rights, the publisher prepares one that calls for transfer of the author's copyright ownership in return for a stated compensation.

Permissions

The matter of permissions often comes up during the agreement stage of manuscript processing. The licensing or copyright agreement with the author does not cover items the author borrowed from another source. The editor or author may have to secure separate permission to use them. Typical borrowings may be a few lines of a song, quotations from literary works, an illustration from another work, or a long passage of text, such as a list. An editor hopes that the author has identified all borrowings as such. The basic author-publisher agreement should require the author to do so. Yet every year one reads of a respected writer who has "inadvertently" lifted dozens of passages from another author without credit or permission.

Permissions are required only for certain copyrighted material, and only the copyright owner can grant it. Materials in the public domain may be borrowed freely, but such sources are usually credited as a courtesy or to give the reader valuable source information. It is legal to borrow from material in the public domain without even a credit, as long as there is no attempt to deceive the consumer. Charges of fraud could be brought against works marketed as original but based largely on borrowed material. One such item would be a tax guide marketed as "unique" (and sold at $25) but based entirely on a government publication (available for $1.50).

The new copyright law (see Chapter 7) allows for certain, limited "fair use" of copyrighted material without permission. Fair use of brief excerpts commonly takes place in media of criticism, analysis, and news reporting. For these purposes, editors can usually borrow up to three-hundred words of prose (or a picture) before the copyright proprietors will holler. If the original work is short, however, three-hundred words may be too substantial a portion to use without permission. Proprietors of song lyrics and poems will howl—or sue—over even a line fragment. The key principle in fair use is that the borrower not diminish the marketability of the original by offering too much of it in the new work. Whether an editor wants to exercise what seems like fair use or ask permission for a borrowed item may be influenced by other factors, among them close deadlines, a proprietor who is certain to say no to any request, or the context into which the borrowed material falls: In criticism, for example, a sterling review is far less likely to provoke a challenge to fair use than is a hatchet job.

When in doubt about fair use, it may be well to request permission. It rarely seems worth the time and fuss, especially for a few lines. But if it isn't fair use, then it may be copyright infringement—and that's trouble.

Some published works give limited or even unlimited borrowing permission near the copyright statement or elsewhere in the front matter. One such work is a booklet* issued by the

---

Photocopying by Academic, Public, and Nonprofit Research Libraries, May 1978. Appendix E, cited above, is from an AAP publication, "Explaining the New Copyright Law" and applies as well to permission for reprinting as to permission for photocopying.

Association of American Publishers and the Authors League of America. It states on its cover, "This Document May Be Reproduced Without Permission." Accepting the offer, I am reproducing here part of an appendix entitled, "How to Obtain Permissions."

After checking to determine who owns the copyright on the material, the next step is to request permission to [reprint]. . . . One of the most frequent reasons cited by permissions departments for delays in answering requests . . . is incomplete or inaccurate information contained in requests. A survey of permissions professionals conducted by the AAP determined that the following facts are necessary in order to authorize duplication [or reprinting] of copyrighted materials.

1. Title, author and/or editor, and edition of materials to be duplicated
2. Exact material to be used, giving amount, page numbers, chapters and, if possible, a photocopy of the material
3. Number of copies to be made [total circulation]
4. Use to be made of duplicated materials [e.g., "sidebar to article"]
5. Form of distribution . . . [e.g., "35,000 domestic, 2,000 overseas subscriptions, and approximately 20,000 newsstand sales"]
6. Whether or not the material is to be sold [or profit/nonprofit status of requesting publisher]
7. Type of reprint [e.g., "two-page insert on heavy stock"]

The request should be sent, together with a self-addressed return envelope, to the permissions department of the publisher in question. If the address of the publisher does not appear at the front of the material, it may be readily obtained in publications entitled *The Literary Marketplace* (for books) or *Ulrich's International Periodicals* (for journals), published by the R. R. Bowker Company and available in all libraries.

Because each request must be checked closely by the publisher, it is advisable to allow enough lead time to obtain the permission before the materials are needed. Granting of a permission . . . is not simply a "yes" or "no" matter. (Although many publishers have a minimum or no-charge policy for . . . noncommercial organizations, they might first review the status of the copyright to see if the power to grant . . . rights of this nature is within their scope or province.) Each such request requires a careful checking of the status of copyright, determination of exact materials to be duplicated (which sometimes involves ordering a copy of the material from a warehouse), and assignment of author's royalties if fees are involved. Some helpful hints from those involved daily in the processing of permission include:

1. Request all permissions for a specific project at the same time
2. Don't ask for a blanket permission—it cannot, in most cases, be granted
3. Send a photocopy of the copyright page and the page or pages on which permission is requested .
4. Make sure to include a return address in your request

If the requester represents a small, noncommercial publication, permission editors will sometimes waive the formal process, waive the fees, and insist only that the proper credit be given. Benign permission editors will even give permission over the phone, asking that the requester follow up in writing.

In the worst situations, the permissions process will run past your deadlines, the fee will be outrageous, and the required wording for credits will take up practically as much room as the material being borrowed. Before reaching a point of no return in the production cycle, an editor must decide whether the borrowed material is worth the time and money it will take to get it.

3. *Organization*. This third step in processing a manuscript may be simple and obvious, but it is crucial if some trace of order is to prevail over the remaining steps. When the publisher-author contract is signed and the necessary permissions have been acquired, these documents, or copies of them, are placed with the manuscript and its file of accompanying materials. This file is organized to include:

Editorial notes made during the selection process.

The full correspondence between author and editors, including late author revisions and insertions.

Biographical notes on the author and, if commonly used, an author photo.

Illustrations to accompany the text. If the illustrations are filed elsewhere or not yet received, a reference to them should appear in this main file.

Materials for possible sidebars, boxes, companion pieces, etc.

4. *Assignment*. As the issue for which the manuscript has been scheduled draws near, the editor-in-chief assigns to an appropriate staffer the responsibility of copy editing—i.e., of shaping that massive, amorphous file of materials into a clean, concise, wholly accurate, and evocative presentation for the readers. Chief editors may choose to take on this responsibility themselves or assign it to a part-time or freelance copy editor. The editor taking on the assignment now performs or oversees the remaining steps.

5. *Review*. The first—and one of the most neglected—duties of the copy editor is to *read and re-read every item in the manuscript file*. This file—which may be a single, bulging folder—contains scraps and chits scribbled in the heat of deadlines and rammed in with the other materials in no particular order. It is typical for one such scrap to say, "Author called this a.m.—says he misspelled Stien throughout ms. Should be Stein." Or something like, "Stein's lawyer called late p.m. Says she won't sue if we remove the next-to-last footnote." And so on. Horror stories abound in my memory—of the editor who painstakingly edited the original manuscript instead of the revised one a few items down in the file; or of the wrong illustrations used because instructions in the author's correspondence were never noted; or of such oversights as omitted permission and copyright credits and outdated biographical information.

6. *Measurement and typesetting specification*. Manuscript length and choice of typefaces are interrelated. The editor must know how many pages of print, in this typeface or that, the text will occupy so that the proper space can be reserved in the

issue's dummy. The editor does a rough word count, never relying on the author's count. The latter is often nothing more than the editor's specified maximum, preceded by the word "approximately." The author is saying, "I didn't count it, but I hope it's not more than you asked for." Nine out of ten authors write beyond the maximum. It is far more time-consuming to write short.

Of course, the length should have been made to conform to the editor's plans before the piece was accepted; but very often the extra length read well, or later revisions and addenda slipped into the file unmeasured. Now the editor must decide how much will be cut or added so that a typeface and column width can be chosen and the piece edited to fit a fixed number of pages. Sometimes that number has been determined already, based on earlier estimates, the size of other pieces running in the same issue, placement of advertisements, or standard sizes of departments. A more flexible publication might make up its final dummy only after the pieces have been set in type, allowing the length of the articles-as-edited to determine the layout of the issue. As a result, whole departments may have to be dropped or hauled out of back files to accommodate unexpected lengths.

The typeface, too, may be predetermined by the standard design of the magazine and its departments. If not, the editor chooses an appropriate "form" to follow the function and content of the manuscript—say, an authoritative 10-point Times Roman with 2 points of leading on a 20-pica column for a lofty statement of national policy.

Knowing the typeface and column size and the number of words in the manuscript, the editor can apply the formulas for copy-sizing and come up with a length-in-print.* If the text

---

*For example, approximately 1,910 words in 10-point Times Roman, 2 points leading, on a 20-pica column at a (known) 450 words per 9-inch column equals 1,910 divided by 450, or 4.24 columns. The total columns of type (4.24) divided by the number of columns per page (say, 2) equals approximately 2½ pages of text.

measures out to, say, two-and-a-half pages, and three are available, the editor either trims the article to a two-pager and informs the appropriate staff that a page has been freed, or goes for three pages by means of the next step:

7. *Illustration and layout planning*. To enhance the text as much as to fill out the available space, the editor now considers the illustrations, captions, heads, blowups, white space, and other design elements that will be needed. On some magazines the graphic considerations are largely the province of the art editor. On others, art and copy editors will work back and forth in shaping these elements. And on many small publications, one editor will do it all—and sweep up afterward. But whatever the arrangement, the illustrations must be assigned no later than at this point. The editors study the manuscript to form the illustration concepts, determine size, then make the necessary assignments to secure the illustrations on time. They may draw upon a staff photographer or artist, an art studio or independent freelancer, or in-house or commercial picture archives.

8. *Styling and copy editing*. Now comes line-by-line editing of the manuscript, a step that is often confused with the whole of the editorial process. In a typical magazine operation, the editor who is assigned the manuscript will make a copy of the original and go to work on it with pencil, scissors, and tape—or video display terminal (VDT) keyboard. The scraps in the folder, the author's revisions and additions, and the boxes and sidebars are brought together in an appealing order, and word by word, line by line, wherever necessary for the reader's benefit, the text is pruned and polished. (See Chapters 3 and 4.)

In addition to editing for clarity, economy, logic, and impact, the copy editor routinely:

• Sees that punctuation, spelling, figures, capitalization, etc., conform to the house style;
• Double-checks the accuracy of names, titles, citations, and mathematical computations;

- Writes the author's biographical note and, if necessary, editor's notes;
- Writes titles, heads, and subheads—rarely using those provided by the author;
- Writes a "teaser" line or two (also called a "deck," or "blurb") to accompany the title and pull readers into the article (for example, "The three unsafest airlines are the last most travelers would guess");
- Specifies ("specs") the typeface and size for all these elements as well as for the main text.

9. *Typesetting*. More and more publications are copy editing at least some text directly on video display terminals. In an integrated, on-line system, the editorial VDT units can exchange data with other units and send instructions electronically; the editor hits a few keys and transmits the edited, type-spec'd, and file-coded copy to the typesetting component, which will soon deliver galleys. In off-line systems, a disk or a tape will be taken to the typesetting component.

In the more traditional setup, with editing done on paper, the copy editor sends the marked-up, numbered manuscript pages to the typesetting department or service. Some advanced systems call for cleanly typed and marked copy, which will be scanned by an optical character recognition (OCR) device. The OCR scan converts the text and instructions into digital signals for automated typesetting.

10. *Proofreading and layout*. The manuscript processing is complete when the proofread galleys, illustrations, captions, heads, and other related elements are joined together physically into page layouts comprising an integrated whole, which—one always hopes—will be considerably greater than the sum of its parts. Whether the final product is to be a lush two-page spread in an art magazine or a frame of videotext news on a home computer/television system, the key to its effectiveness lies as much in the editorial process as in the process of its creation.

Creativity Within the Basic Steps

As noted earlier in this chapter, the editorial "process" exists only to assure that a particular result will come about consistently and economically. Without process, what comes in as chaos would remain chaos. Dadaists may prefer such editorial anarchy to order; but most publishers and readers do like to see something in the way of a result or "product."

The process, however, should never become so overwhelming as to create unalterable patterns and smother editorial initiative. Each editor brings unique enhancements to the meaning of "editing." These individualized approaches distinguish and enliven a medium. When a publisher discourages them, the product usually shows it.

Today we see dozens of publications "processed" with assembly-line uniformity. Let us call one of them *Ennui* magazine. We know the look. For *Ennui* editors, processing a manuscript means breaking the text into spoon-sized paragraphs, adding a buzzword-laden title, a tantalizing subtitle, an italic note to tie the manuscript to the issue's larger themes, a dazzling subhead every half column, a forceful bleed illustration, a shocking blowup quote, and a cute closing dingbat to seal in the effervescence. Is anyone still awake?

Why are some publications edited by formula? Perhaps the publisher paid a fashionable editorial consultant to cast the mold, and to break it would be a waste of money. Perhaps the editors are androids, programmed only to replicate other formula publications. Whatever the cause, every issue as well as every article of the *Ennuis* begin to look the same, and readers have trouble remembering which they have and have not taken on. Eventually, they no longer care.

3

Editor and Writer

AN UNEASY ALLIANCE

EDITORS NEED WRITERS and have been known to end up liking a few. But editors are also foot soldiers in the eternal war between raw talent and the people who process that talent. As long as writers write primarily to advance themselves, and editors edit to satisfy readers, there will never be a lasting peace.

An editor's only permanent alliance is with the audience, the readership. It is the editor's responsibility to hook that readership; to edify it, entertain it, stroke it, shake it up—do whatever is necessary to keep the medium hot and desirable for the people who support it.

The editor, not the author, best understands that readership. Authors know their subject. Editors specialize in knowing the audience. They live with it week to week; they ponder reader correspondence; they analyze the groups and subgroups making up the readership; and they study the spectrum of success and failure among media serving this audience. Because an editor's self-esteem and very job depend on satisfying readers, it is the reader, not the author, who will receive first consideration when conflicts of interest arise.

A good editor will fight to the death even against the almighty publisher if the readers are being abused; and any editor who can stand up to the moguls who sign the paychecks will make short work of self-serving, recalcitrant authors.

Who's in Charge?

Too many new editors are afraid to say no, especially to established writers and other authorities. And it is dreadfully intimidating when, say, a U.S. senator writes six thousand words over your maximum on his national health plan and refuses to cut one line; or when a celebrated actress wishes to insert a diatribe on whale slaughter into her interview; or your best advertiser submits a puff piece on a slow-moving product; or the executive editor hand-delivers a cover design executed by her out-of-work husband ("It would mean so much to his morale if you could use this!"). Every day, in almost every situation, there is pressure to compromise commitment to reader interest in favor of some other cause—and not always an unworthy one.

An editor must be flexible enough to realize that reader interest can be served in various ways and that some trade-offs are worth considering. But the line is drawn when a compromise results in a net loss for the consumer of the media product: in more that is dull, irrelevant, and downright hostile to the reader than is compelling, informative, and gratifying. Editors may get away with such compromises here and there, but an accumulation of them will surely result in a reader rebellion without mercy.

To appeal to the readers' interest does not mean to salute their every prejudice. No editor should make that mistake. Readers of even the schlockiest fanzine or most rabid political journal are at least as interested in being challenged as being stroked. But the challenge should be to their beliefs, not to their patience.

Another common mistake is to challenge the readers' ability to make connections existing in the editor's mind, not on the page. Do I illustrate an article on summer salads with a portrait of Cesar Chavez, hoping that my feelings about California lettuce will come across? This sort of approach is not challenging readers but testing them, and the difference is crucial.

Telling the Author What's Best

An editor enters the combat zone armed with clear-cut criteria for publication. Based on editorial goals and reader priorities, these criteria are the first measure of an author's work. All other considerations—who the author is, who will be impressed if the manuscript is published, who will be crushed if it is not—are secondary. An editor who can point to a set of criteria worked out intelligently to serve the medium's audience is in the best position to resist pressures from authors, publishing executives, and others with special interests.

Good, clear criteria also help editors choose the most publishable manuscripts from among several outstanding contenders. And, when used as guidelines during the editing process, established criteria protect the editor from charges of arbitrariness in revising the author's text.

Any list of standards, of course, is an ideal, and must not be followed slavishly. The criteria must be organic, subject to review, and moderated by the editor's gut feelings.

Below is an adaptation of criteria I developed for a monthly magazine serving a professional association. Criteria will vary according to type of magazine and audience, but general qualities such as originality, clarity, and force will always be sought.

Criteria for Evaluating Manuscripts

The following may be kept in mind as a general approach to evaluating manuscripts for publication, or they may be used as a quantitative rating system for choosing between manuscripts close in overall quality. (For the latter use, score each of the ten aspects from 1 to 100 points. Rating of each manuscript by at least two editors is recommended.) Finally, the criteria may serve as guidelines for editorial revisions of an author's text.

CONTENT

1. *Information*. Delivers a body of facts. Resources are authoritative. Original-research methods are competent. Opinions are supported by information.

2. *Analysis and interpretation*. The facts are organized and examined, not merely enumerated. Concepts or hypotheses are presented that embody the facts and bear the imprint of the author. Difficult concepts are made manageable. Thoughtful interpretation leads one to a pointed overview of the subject. Knowledge (a synthesis of information) as well as raw information is imparted. The article is substantially more than the sum of its sources.

3. *Balance*. Opinions are clearly distinguished from fact. More than one side of an argument is presented or at least acknowledged. The reader has a fair chance to judge the reliability of the information.

4. *Originality*. Fresh, innovative, insightful. Shows an awareness of earlier thoughts on the subject, as well as an ability to go beyond them.

READABILITY

5. *Appeal*. From the start, the article is inviting. It intrigues or motivates the reader; it encourages one to go beyond the first page. It sustains interest throughout. Its organization creates a forward momentum. It contains a succession of interesting facts and concepts clearly presented. An authoritative command of the subject promises substantial educational value.

6. *Concreteness and clarity.* It favors the concrete over the abstract. It is free of jargon and turgid rhetoric. It gets to the point. It specifies. It asserts its point of view. It invites dialogue. It offers concrete points of reader identification. It rings with clarity.

7. *Color and tone.* The voice is conversational but intelligent. It favors active over passive construction, sentences that build on strong verbs. It uses, when appropriate, examples, anecdotes, contrast, irony, and wit. Expression is sincere rather than slick. In general, the writing is free of elements that intrude upon the smooth flow of information and ideas to the reader.

IMPACT

8. *Enlightenment.* Edifies without preaching. Opens up new channels of action or understanding. Leaves one with a sense of solid benefit. Emotionally as well as intellectually stimulating. Turns on the inner light.

9. *Force.* Authoritative and persuasive without heavy-handedness. Intensity of conviction, strength of logic. Shows an awareness of trends, but does not derive its impact from ephemeral fashions and follies. Durable.

10. *Relevance.* The article relates directly to current or enduring interests of the specific readership. It rewards, extends, or challenges these interests.

Copy Editing: Hand-to-Hand Combat

Much of your time as an editor is devoted to fighting off authors and other people who want you to publish something that doesn't live up to your criteria, doesn't make it on its own merits. Saying no to all these people is part of editorial combat, but usually not the bloodiest. The real trench warfare is fought with authors to whom you have said yes: Yes, we will accept your article, book, script, whatever, under certain conditions.

One of these conditions, spelled out in writing if possible, must be that the author submit to or cooperate in a reasonable amount of copy editing. No author on this planet is so attuned to your audience that every word, every comma, in the manuscript can be accepted as inviolable. Yet there are grim stories in every editorial office about writers who have demanded immunity from revision or have resisted every least change with a ferocity to be envied by killer bees.

One cannot always generalize about which types of writers most despise editorial revision, but in this editor's experience it has not been the established writers. John Galbraith and Nat Hentoff, for example, come to mind as two who were perfectly amenable to changes, while obscure academics were "shocked" to see two paragraphs transposed or "appalled" that an English spelling was changed to American. On the other hand, a *Time* report (September 1, 1980) noted that for an increasing number of authors, success does indeed seem to spoil appreciation of the editing process. Why should I let them change a word, the bestselling author reasons, when they thought my words were worth so much money?

The truth is, an editor doesn't always think a raw manuscript is worth very much. What attracts an editor to it in the selection process often is its *potential* for being shaped into a successful product for the audience. But most authors, in their artistic integrity, cringe at the notion of being "shaped" into a consumer "product."

Who is right? The reader-oriented editor or the reputation-oriented author? Certainly there is nothing intrinsically evil about the author's desire to keep by-lined material true to the original heartfelt intent and style, to have a voice in deciding which cuts and additions are made, and to manifest personal feelings about grammar and rhetoric rather than submit to an editor's stylebook. But all these concerns can conflict with the editor's legitimate goals.

Some lines of fair play can be drawn, but lightly. A manuscript's *content*, most editors will agree, is the author's province; the author knows the subject or would not have made the sale. But the *form* of the final product—its organization, pace, packaging—is what editors like to think is their specialty. If an editor first explains this dichotomy and shows respect for an author's knowledge of a subject, the author might yield agreeably to the editor's expertise in matters of form.

My own plea to authors goes something like this: "Now, Dr. Einstein, you've spent a lifetime contemplating the properties of the universe, and I've spent most of my life communicating complex ideas to average people. As long as my revision doesn't change your meaning, won't you allow me my craft of editing?" I am amazed at how often this type of appeal will resolve a conflict—though it surely helps if one's medium enjoys a good reputation for accuracy and integrity.

An author's greatest fear is to appear, as a result of revision, less than brilliant. The good editor convinces authors that *without* revision their genius will be obscured.

"Communication," I recently told a class of writers, "is your reason for being—not nourishment of ego, not praise of colleagues, not money, not love of generations to come. You write to communicate to the hearts and minds of others what's burning inside you—

"And we edit to let the fire show through the smoke."

Thought Control: An Editorial War Crime

Ideally the war between editors and authors should be won by neither belligerent, but by the readers. The readers are served best when the editor has preserved the author's strengths and eliminated only the weaknesses in communication.

Unfortunately, most editors, new and seasoned, do not play by all the rules of this benign war. The little poster below is one I put up for my editorial staff the day I first saw it:

> The strongest drive
>
> is not love or hate.
>
> It is one person's need
>
> ~~modify, revise alter~~
>
> to ~~change~~ another's copy.
>
> ~~rewrite amend~~
>
> change ~~chop to pieces~~

All too true. The first impulse we have with another's copy is to make it *sound* right, and what sounds right to us is our own voice, our own idiom. Also, the more we change another's copy, the more we seem to justify our own editorial importance, perhaps even our job. Sometimes office politics plays a part in heavy-handed editing. The second editor along the line must show how incompetent the first editor was by finding a dozen more "corrections," all of thcm arbitrary.

These are motives editors can learn to recognize and purge. Revisions motivated by an editor's disagreement with an author's ideas are more difficult to track and moderate. We are all pledged to defend to the death the author's right to disagreeable ideas; but some of us cannot resist the urge to "defeat" this odious author—to practice editing-as-confrontation, even to subvert some of the author's ideas in the name of moral, intellectual, or artistic superiority.

The line must be drawn. An editor's job is to shape the *expression* of an author's thoughts, not the thoughts themselves. The editor deletes jargon, redundancies, and irrelevancies— never ideas, unless the author consents. Sometimes the author's voice is an integral part of a thought and must be preserved, even if it is loathsome to the editorial ear.

To summarize, the good editor is methodical and merciless in rejecting unsatisfactory copy; discriminating in editing out weaknesses and enhancing strengths of an author's text; and compassionate in preserving the author's original ideas. The good editor has the confidence to say no to any author who would compromise the medium's standards, and the humility to recognize when those standards are transcended.

For all the toughness of the editorial hide, a soft spot will always be found for the honest writer—the type described by Editor Anthony Prete as people who "continue to write, many of them with no assurance that their words will ever appear in print," but who are determined "to share, to enlighten, to entertain."

Prete continues:

For me, such determination reflects what is finest in human nature. . . . It takes pride and a strong sense of self to write for publication, to tell the world (or a small part thereof) that we think our ideas are important, our experiences valuable—even at the risk of being contradicted, ridiculed, or ignored. Writers make themselves vulnerable the same way good teachers do: by taking what is innermost (an insight, an affection, an encounter) and exposing it to public view, struggling to make it as precise, as poignant, as persuasive as possible. For some it is a form of martyrdom, for others, masochism; for most, it is an irrepressible necessity.*

With these writers, we form an alliance, uneasy as it might be.

*Anthony Prete, "In Focus: Ten Cents a Book." *Media & Methods*, November 1978.

4

The Agony and the Agony
LINE EDITORS AND THEIR CRAFT

"Great qualities are too precarious when left to themselves, un-steadied and unballasted by knowledge, abandoned to mere im-pulse and untutored daring; they need the bridle as well as the spur."
–Longinus, *On the Sublime*

"EDITING SO-AND-SO'S MANUSCRIPT was a *pleasure*," I once heard a staffer remark. There must have been laughing gas in the air. Going over a manuscript line by line has as little to do with pleasure as does the creation of those lines. More impor-tant is that the reader be pleased by the result. If the author gains millions, and the editor a fleeting moment of satisfaction, fine. But the editing itself is an excruciating act of self-disci-pline, mind-reading, and stable-cleaning. If it seems like a pleasure, something is probably wrong.

A line-by-line editing assignment may befall any staffer from junior-level up. Routinely, associate-level, "line," or copy editors will be assigned a raw manuscript. Chief, managing, and senior editors get involved when the story or author is important enough or the firm small. Beginning editors may be assigned line editing of regular departments or be called into action for larger scripts when the desks, chairs, and windows are piled high with editing backlogs.

When editors breeze through forty pages in an hour or eight hundred in a week, I worry that they have not undergone the agonies prerequisite to launching someone's words into eternity. I begin to ask annoying questions:

Have they weighed every phrase and sentence of the script to determine whether the author's meaning will be carried to the intended audience?

Have they measured every revision they propose to make against the advantages of the author's original voice and presentation?

Have they pondered the effectiveness of every phrase to the limits of their grammatical ear—and then beyond, with two or three modern-usage guides at hand?

Have they studied every possible area of numerical, factual, or judgmental error until they can swear that to the best of their knowledge and research this manuscript is accurate and ready to be immortalized in print?

Have they strained their eyes for typos and transpositions, especially in those parts of the manuscript retyped or reorganized? Have they edited and proofread their own editing as well?

Have they—or the proofreaders whose work they manage—groveled in the details of the footnotes, tables, and appendices until every last em-dash, en-dash, and subscript is marked, every parenthesis is closed, and all abbreviations and italicizations are consistent?

Have they cast a legal eye upon every quoted phrase, defamatory comment, trade name, allegation, and attribution, whether it appears in footnote, caption, dedication, title page, or main text?

Have they stepped back to consider the impact of the whole as well as the parts, tuned an ear to overtones of sexism, racism, ageism, ethnocentrism, and any other isms that will undermine the intentions of author and publisher or unintentionally alienate the reader?

Have they, if required, provided all the editorial embellishments to the text—title, subtitle, subheads, author notes, editorial notes, sidebars, blowups, dingbats, and instructions to the designer?

Have they, if it is the policy of the publication, cleared every significant revision and addition with the author?

Editors who can do all this in a twinkling are either in league with the devil or as one with the gods. But I've never met such an editor, nor any humanoid who can singlehandedly convert an author's raw copy into a flawlessly clean manuscript, however much time is available. Consummate editing requires a team of at least two: an in-depth editor, and what might be called a "quality-control" editor to provide a check on the collaborative effort of author and first editor. Where deadlines inhibit this level of editing, as on fast-breaking news media, the product shows it. In reading the morning newspaper, I give thanks every other paragraph that these garbled stories aren't about me. The infamous 1981 Pulitzer Prize hoax at the *Washington Post* underscored the dilemma of 24-hour cycles. "If you have a rule that makes an editor check every single fact," said *Post* editor Ben Bradlee, "you are going to put out a monthly newspaper."

If line editing (or "micro-editing," as some call it) is such agony and no one seems able to master it, why do so many intelligent people take it on? I suppose for the challenge and unpredictability of the work. Those who can't climb Mount Everest find happiness in tackling the barriers to clear expression. One never knows what those barriers will be; the variety is infinite. The only predictable element in editing is that the next problem to come along will not yield to any of the thousands of solutions developed in tackling previous problems.

The Ecstasy and Agony of an Editor's Education

One prepares to be a line editor simply by mastering the world's knowledge, the specialized knowledge of one's audience, and the craft of working with words. The broader one's learning, the greater the ability to identify errors, distortions, embarrassments, calumnies, idiocies, and barbarisms before they appear in print to discredit the publication—or worse. The compleat line editor can spot a faulty classical allusion in an article on the Nauruan phosphate industry as well as a transposed subscript in $Ca_3(PO_4)_2$, a dangling participle in the lead sentence, and a libelous crack about a plant manager.

To learn about the world beyond one's subject specialization, one reads widely. Travel helps, as do acquaintances from many fields and a broad range of cultural, intellectual, and romantic interests. But the basic lifelong education of an editor is reading—reading everything and anything at every opportunity. Reading to satisfy one's bizarre curiosities, serendipitous reading, literary reading, informational reading, course reading, work-related reading, and escape reading.

The special skill of the line editor is working with words. A mastery of good syntax—how words are strung together well—can come in only two ways: by spending the first twenty-five years of one's life in a drawing room with E. B. White, Vladimir Nabokov, Elizabeth Bowen, Gabriel García Márquez, Saul Bellow, Eudora Welty, John Fowles, Langston Hughes, Joyce Carol Oates, James Baldwin, and John Updike—or by reading their works and those of other writers whose choice of words and word arrangement establishes our standards of literate communication.

An ingrained ear for language comes from reading good literature and balances the domestic babble, street talk, advertising drivel, and work jargon ravaging our brains.

Somewhere, every day, someone laments the decline of American literacy. We hear that many a Civil War foot soldier wrote more elegant prose than our average university professor, or that the forthcoming generations may revert to grunts, sign language, and pictographs as they turn away from reading. Yet it seems that more people than ever care about language, at least as evidenced by the mass-media offerings on the subject, language columnists, bestselling books on better writing, and thousands of line editors being paid to make prose communicate and make it—as they used to insist at *Time*—sing.

"Literary judgment," said Longinus seventeen centuries ago, "is the last outgrowth of long experience." Similarly, nothing substitutes for the sense of good language that comes from years of reading good writers and, if one is lucky enough, being around people who speak well. Often, new editorial staffers have an ear for language based on what they call, defensively, "the way everyone talks," which means the habitual patterns in which their families and hometown friends talk—not the special language of words that must communicate precisely and accurately, please, and persuade; of words that must stand up to the scrutiny of knowledgeable readers, listeners, or viewers; of words that must earn a certain amount of money to pay for their very costly packaging and distribution.

Not having developed a highly literate ear, some beginning editors are most frustrated by questions of diction (choice of words) and idiom. When one such editor revises "What price justice?" to read, "How much are we supposed to pay for justice?" it isn't easy to explain why the original is preferable. "Yes, it's shorter," says the new editor, "but it doesn't mean anything. Even if the verb 'to be' is understood, the thought is incomplete." The thought, I try to indicate, is completed by a thousand echoes of this idiom from previous literary uses—echoes that are lost, along with the feelings they evoke, in the revision.

"Show me the rule," the editor demands. "Where is the rule covering echoes?"

Sometimes in a book of style or rhetoric (the art of using

language effectively) I can point to a literary device behind certain idiomatic expressions. But the only general rule I can prescribe for editors with a pedestrian ear is to enroll in a Great Books program.

If there is an art to line editing, it is probably this literate ear and the ability to apply it when appropriate. It is similar to the composer's feeling, acquired from thousands of hours of listening to good music, for what constitutes that indefinable term "classical."

An editor named Blair McElroy writes that, in editing, "whatever changes you make should be for accuracy, clarity, felicity, or just plain intelligibility." The art of editing has most to do with felicity—with making just the right improvement to create light, joy, song, aptness, grace, beauty, or excitement where it wasn't quite happening. The rest—improving accuracy, clarity, and general intelligibility—may be thought of as the craft of line editing.

The Crafty Editor

The craft, in turn, may be seen as a number of skills. So that we may all enumerate them when seeking raises, I offer this breakdown: research, strategy, perception, organization, language, and troubleshooting.

In Chapter 6 I discuss research, the *sine qua non* of accuracy. Troubleshooting is explored in Chapter 5. Chapters 2 and 3 treat large-scale editorial strategy—for example, how to organize the manuscript project and deal effectively with authors. Here the focus is on the actual text, line by line.

Strategy means identifying the goals of the line-editing job and planning how to achieve them in the time available. It is a skill acquired by experience and self-discipline, for the first impulse of most editors is to plunge into a manuscript and start revising it without a thought of why or how much. With experience, however, comes these realizations:

—Some manuscripts are going to be read mainly for their

"hard" data, and so require more attention to fact than to beauty; others require an opposite editorial emphasis.

—Some manuscripts are so badly in need of revision that the author must be called upon to prepare another draft. If the editor attempts an elaborate, page-by-page revision and eventually decides the job is getting out of hand, it may be too late to go back or forward.

—Frequently the manuscript should be broken up into smaller elements: a three-part series; or a main story and three or four sidebars; or a main text and—in lieu of certain longueurs—illustrations with captions. Such treatments require strategic planning.

—Certain parts of a manuscript may be beyond an editor's technical knowledge. Will the editor have time to bone up on the necessary background, or is another strategy required? Which parts of a manuscript ought to be edited first, the easy or nightmarish ones?

—Finally, there are several levels or "depths" at which any manuscript can be edited. Consonant with the goals of the article and the time available, one must determine the appropriate depth of editing and maintain it throughout the manuscript. The most common failing of inexperienced copy editors is inconsistency in the depth of their work on a given project. They approach a fat manuscript in an attack mode, full of fighting spirit, and completely rewrite the first three pages, carefully checking the accuracy of every revised statement and bringing the prose up to a biblical level. Then, exhausted and short on time, they scan the remaining pages for nothing more than omitted commas and throw the script on the boss's desk with a "Whew!"

What are the levels of editing? "Light, medium, and heavy" have different meanings under varying conditions. Suppose the work to be edited is a six thousand-word manuscript on an unapproachable, world-champion tennis brat. The author is an intimate friend of the athlete and a formidable young foe of English. My first impulse would be to seize the article's best observations and, in my own prose, create a sports profile so dazzling as to be anthologized for the next 50 years. Instead, resisting that urge, I plan my level of editing according to the time I have available for the job. Perhaps something like this:

One day: Correct spelling and the worst grammatical errors; style according to house rules of punctuation, numbers, capitalization, etc.; resolve inconsistencies; check any statements that seem absurd or actionable.

Two days: In addition to the above, rework some of the prose to make it more active and concrete; cut or shift a few paragraphs to create a powerful opening and logical development. Spot-check one or two sources (the brat himself, if possible) to be sure they are being quoted accurately.

Three days: In addition, rewrite some of the weakest passages, establishing a momentum that keeps the reader going; carefully cut any passages interfering with this momentum and provide the necessary transition; check as many facts as possible with resources at hand or nearby. Thoroughly re-read the revised manuscript and judge it against the author's original tone and intent, conferring with the author if there are serious differences and with an attorney if legal questions remain.

Strategic skills, then, enable the line editor to tackle the manuscript as a whole, concentrate time and energy where they count most in achieving editorial goals, plan for the extraordinary and the troublesome, and make deadlines.

Perception for editors means hearing what the author is trying to say while keeping an ear tuned to the sensibilities of the readers.

Listening to the author requires empathy and a suppression of ego. One of the most obnoxious traits of editors is to superimpose their own perceptions upon the author's imperfectly completed thoughts. Certainly we don't behave this boorishly in conversation:

"I find this gathering so—so—"

"So arid?"

"No, I mean so—"

"So infantile?"

"No, I mean so *stimulating*, you deadhead!"

Communications instructors often lead classroom experiments to show how utterly rotten most of us are at perception. We manage to tune out practically everything that does not reinforce our attitudes or satisfy an immediate emotional or intellectual need. Another theory holds that blurred perception derives from our eagerness to "help." People want to solve a problem, not really hear what a person is saying and feeling.

One can spell out the techniques of good listening at textbook length; but editors who make an ironclad commitment to hearing out their authors will fare well enough. When all else fails, such editors will not hesitate to pick up the telephone, dial an author's number, and ask: "What on earth did you *mean* when you said . . . ?"

Stalking the Elusive Reader

Listening to readers has less to do with concentration than with data gathering, analysis, and sometimes years of legwork. Who are the readers? What do they want? What do they need? What turns them on and off? What is *relevant* to them? To answer these ancient questions, media producers have exploited every tool from market research to the *I Ching*, sometimes with satisfying short-range results. But because people change, do not always know their own needs, and don't like to reveal what they do know about themselves, there *are* no long-range answers. Thus the Nielsen ratings must be taken every week, and publishers schedule periodic market research.

The smaller and more specialized an audience, the easier it is to identify certain of its interests and attitudes. Those joining the Lepidopterist's Book Club want regular helpings of butterflies and moths. But mass audiences also behave in patterns, some of which can be tracked by market analysis.

One form of analysis is the readership survey, which many editors feel is a waste of time. Self-surveys (those distributed with the publication) addressed to the full readership tend to draw most answers from an atypical segment: the highly motivated, involved, attentive readers. These readers may encourage editors to expand the heady sections, while the silent majority quietly switches to a medium with better sports coverage. Surveys that take a "scientifically selected" sampling or one that is painstakingly random come up with answers supposedly typical of the full readership. But editors are uncomfortable making major decisions based on so few respondents; or, by the time they get comfortable, they can argue that the readership has changed.

Some of the most famous success stories are those of editors who represented themselves as "the average intelligent reader" and went no further than their own tastes in researching the preferences of the audience. But for every such success story (*Scientific American*'s is one of them), there are probably dozens of uncelebrated fiascos.

Other sources of information about readers include their letters to the editor and to other in-house departments, their response to your advertisers, and their preferences among offerings of competing media. Whichever sources are used, the editors must eventually hear an identifiable reader voice or make their complex, crucial decisions in a vacuum.

Soon after Carll Tucker became editor of the *Saturday Review*, he noted that "insensitivity to the needs or tastes of the reader can result in instant disaffection, loss of circulation, and defection of advertisers. . . . " But he reminded us that, "while editors must be sensitive to the opinions of readers, they must not be intimidated by them."*

Butter Out of Chaos

In line editing, *organizational* skills have to do with which lines best go where; and the notion "best" usually boils down to

*Carll Tucker, "Our Curious Business," *Saturday Review*, November 12, 1977, p. 64.

"most logical" and "most interesting" for the target audience. Often the best place for lines to go is directly into the wastebasket. One notorious editor at *The New Yorker* used to hack away the first two or three paragraphs of almost any manuscript brought before him, declaring, "This will cut like butter." His manner was nasty, but the deletion usually made sense. Labored, repugnant openings are pandemic in the writing trade, for most authors hate to cut these or any other lines born of creative agony. One of the editor's most important organizational skills is to recognize the malignant, functionless portions of a text and perform the necessary surgery without damaging the healthy tissue. Where a surgeon uses a scalpel, an editor employs blue pencil, scissors, and paste—or the delete, transpose, and resequence functions of an editing VDT. Like the surgeon, the editor must tie up the loose ends resulting from the excisions. Surgeons call it suturing; we call it transition: smoothing over the cut so that what came before flows smoothly and logically into what came after.

To operate on a manuscript may not require eight years of postgraduate training and malpractice insurance, but there are many ways to butcher the job. The end result sounds simple enough: an inviting beginning, solid middle, and conclusive ending. Yet every author knows the hardships of sticking to an outline—as well as to the principles of economy, unity, coherence, emphasis, consistency, cause-and-effect, and point of view, to name a few elements that affect organization. Ideally, editors ought to acquire a writer's mastery of these elements before tampering with a serious piece of prose. In practice, one learns as one goes along, accumulating numerous tricks of the trade. For example, I often find the perfect beginning for a manuscript in the very last paragraph. Here is where so many authors finally realize exactly why they have written everything that came before; and here they release the information the reader so dearly wanted to know in the first place: *Why am I reading this?*

Organization also calls for some breaking up of the text

before the narrative becomes too tedious. The editor can provide little "intermissions": section breaks, chapter breaks, boxes, sidebars, graphics, some comic relief, and so on. Editors, after all, are impresarios; they are putting on shows they hope will enthrall an audience from start to finish. But they know that a program of even the hottest acts needs skillful pacing.

Grammar: The Line-by-Line Conundrum

English grammar, especially as a reflection of North American usage, has as many cults and priests as there are variations in how educated people express themselves. Sometimes grammar seems not a skill, but a cabala.

It is even difficult to find two similar definitions of grammar; but most are encompassed by Bergen and Cornelia Evans' "a systematic description of the ways in which words are used in a particular language. The grammarian groups words that behave similarly into classes and then draws up rules stating how each class of words behaves."*

Grammar is analytical and nonevaluative. Usage, however, analyzes the status of grammatical patterns within a community, defining "standard," "substandard," and other levels of use.

Standard (or "formal") usually means the way language is used by those community members considered educated and well-spoken. And, oh, if only we could agree on who those members are! Then at last editors would have a sovereign authority to rule on grammatical questions.

We have no such authority, no national language board. What we do have are at least ten thousand educated and well-spoken "experts" with hundreds of thousands of disagreements among them.

For example, the *Harper Dictionary of Contemporary Usage*

*Bergen and Cornelia Evans, *A Dictionary of Contemporary American Usage*, New York, Random House, 1957.

(1975 edition) claims to be "the most authoritative and comprehensive reference book on the state of the language today." Why so authoritative? Because, recognizing rightly that "standard" usage varies according to human experience, it draws upon the advice of 136 outstanding writers and editors, not to mention the wisdom of editors William and Mary Morris. The result *is* an excellent source of advice for editing decisions, one of the best of its kind. But those seeking absolute authority will note that, overall, the 136 writers offer 136 different views on "correct" usage. True, there is general accord on some questions. Only 4 percent of a panel voted yes on using *ain't* in writing, and then only as a matter of style; but a panel voting on *data is* vs. *data are* was split 49 percent for *is*, 51 percent for *are*. One ends up taking the view of favorites on a given panel—or that of W. H. Auden, whose opinion on the *data* question was simply: "I am not sure."

Consensus among usage experts is rare and ephemeral. American English goes through periods of volatile as well as evolutionary change. The experts, too, change their positions, and any group of reigning authorities is as tenuous as a military junta. Small surprise, then, that beginning editors suffer vertigo over "correct" grammar and "standard" usage. One moment they read in the *Harper Dictionary* that "between you and I" is "dreadful illiteracy!" according to Sydney J. Harris and 97 percent of the usage panel; the next moment they learn it is good enough for Shakespeare: "All debts are cleared between you and I"—*The Merchant of Venice*, Act III, Scene 2.

Author Jim Quinn remarks, "Though our popularizers of good grammar think they are defending standards and traditions, they keep attacking idioms that are centuries old." He cites as other venerable and currently maligned usages the construction "anyone can do what *they* want" and the word input. "In the limp and fuzzy rhetoric of pop grammar," he says, " 'illiterate' means 'hasn't read my stylebook.' "★

★Jim Quinn, "Hopefully They Will Shut Up," *Newsweek*, February 23, 1981, p. 9.

And so, lacking a stylebook of imperial authority, many beginning editors either embrace the handiest, holiest-looking old tome, or become anarchists, believing it makes no difference what one decides; someone will find it "wrong."

Those in need of authority may turn to their college or even high-school grammar text, which they have dusted off and rediscovered to be simple and straightforward. Or they will recall the ten unbreakable principles of grammar drummed into them by a revered English instructor ("Number five: *Never* end a sentence with a preposition!"). Theodore M. Bernstein has created a character representing all such instructors: Miss Thistlebottom. In his *Miss Thistlebottom's Hobgoblins* he lays to rest many of the "taboos, bugbears, and outmoded rules of English usage" that the Thistlebottoms instilled in their pupils. As Bernstein admits, the old remembered or rediscovered rules may be as good as any for dealing with the job at hand; but new editors who hold these rules sacred quickly become intolerable to their authors and colleagues. Sometimes they suffer shell shock in their first battle with an intimidating figure who brands them as prissy, inflexible, out of tune with the language of the readership, or just plain mistaken. Such wounded editors may despair of ever again blue-penciling more than a misspelled name.

What, then, are beginning editors to do? Strive to become linguistic popes whose authority may no longer be challenged, or serve humbly at the altar of their authors' and superiors' rules?

All editors need not become fanatics or high priests of the language; but most would do well to wade with some fervor in the Ganges of human expression, analyzing anew the thousands of words that flow each day from friends, family, merchants, government, punkers, rockers, lovers, and literati. To know who uses which words when is the proper study of editors. True, a new staffer can be expected to study only so much on top of the hours at the grindstone each week. Yet editing is a profession, and one mark of professionalism is continuing education. The best time to bone up on grammatical skills is in the early years of editing, when one works closely with manuscripts and the homework is light. As editors rise into managerial positions, what little spare time is available will probably be devoted, between crying jags, to mastering administrative and marketing techniques.

Perhaps the most effective continuing education takes place in the act of line editing, provided we incorporate some sort of self-instruction into the process rather than fly through our manuscripts on a wing and a dictionary. We cannot pretend to be walking—or sedentary—encyclopedias of English usage. The flux of language and our imperfect memories bid us to draw on a small library of language reference guides as we work. Ardent use of these sources over the years is what makes us language "experts," but never so expert as to do without them and edit entirely by ear.

In 1981 a well-established book editor described her approach to the literary "find" of the year, a novel by an English author. "No major scenes needed to be cut or paragraphs moved around," she said. "It was more a question of paying scrupulous attention to theme and language. The author had imagined the entire book perfectly. My job was to ensure that the best words were used, and that the only ambiguities left in the text were ones . . . [the author] intended."*

To "ensure that the best words were used"! Not a job to be done by ear, considering that in publishing circles the author was already being compared to Shakespeare and Sophocles.

In summary, line editors must take the language seriously, but they need not be intimidated by the expanding, shifting universe of grammar and usage. We are all unsure of ourselves; for who can master the devious intricacies of grammar save those who teach them every year or study them to the point of perversity?

---

*"Trade News," *Publishers Weekly*, April 17, 1981, p. 30.

I will confess my own inadequacies. I cannot remember most grammatical terms from one day to the next, though a few—such as "mutation plural" and "loose apposition"—might be worth holding onto. But for the editing I do, I needn't bear in mind the definition of "nominative absolute" or know that in the preceding sentence the word "though" introduces a "concessive clause." I need only stay ahead of my readers, staff, and publisher in how well I grasp the structure and idiom of standard American English. I can do *some* of that by ear, having developed one over the decades, and much of it by referring to my language reference shelf as I edit. I can never become invulnerable to the John Simons, who catch even the Jacques Barzuns in minor slipups, and I don't worry about it.

Reviewing two books on language, William Safire remarked, "The English language is not the King's English, or the grammarian's English, but the English-speaking world's English—to be fought for and fought over by all who find joy in the world of words."*

---

*William Safire, "Word Watchers at Work," *The New York Times Book Review*, May 10, 1981.

5

Troubleshooting

THE EDITOR'S MILLION-DOLLAR TALENT

Robert G. Sugarman, *Consultant**

THE ONE EDITORIAL SKILL that even the most Philistine media executives can appreciate is the ability to sniff out trouble before it gets into print or on the air.

For most publishers, trouble takes the form of horrendous errors, libel, invasion of privacy, plagiarism, obscenity, hoax and fabrication, and copyright infringement. Blessed is the lowly editor who consistently helps authors, senior editors, legal staff, and top administrators avoid some of these woes. Conversely, the line editor whose needless alteration of a phrase leads to a quarter-million-dollar libel action may very well be replaced by a wall hanging in the next year's budget.

---

*Robert G. Sugarman, a member of the New York law firm of Weil, Gotshal, & Manges, specializes in intellectual property law. His generously given advice on matters of law has been applied throughout this chapter. The opinions expressed here, however, along with any faults that might remain, are my own.

—A.P.

The best editors become troubleshooters not to hold on to their jobs, however, but because they are decent human beings who don't want to hurt people by publishing false and damaging material. So they learn how to identify and neutralize such troublesome matter—ideally, without compromising the goals of the medium. They learn how trouble can spring from minute or prodigious causes: a single, careless word or a fundamental misunderstanding. They cultivate a talent for seeing the forest even as they concentrate on the trees.

Simply Horrifying Errors

Errors and insensitivities that have nothing to do with breaking laws can be just as harmful to a publisher as those that unleash damage suits. A term or illustration offensive to, say, an ethnic minority or to women taints a book meant for wide distribution in schools and libraries. Offended individuals and groups devoted to spotting such insensitivities can be counted on to blow the whistle shortly after publication. One or two such stumbles and a publisher can be branded as naive or even racist, and sales can be affected for years. A line editor, as we have said before, must be intensely—no, *philharmonically*—in tune with the thinking and language of the target audience—and sensitive as well to peripheral audiences.

Among minute slipups with easily imagined effects might be an incorrect date in a history text bound for the Texas School Adoption Board; a mislabeled organ in an anatomy; a misspelled word in a dictionary; news of a living person appearing under the obituary heading; or a sponsor's name omitted from credit listings. Not long ago a professional magazine referred to its field's most distinguished leader, a black woman, as Ms. Brown instead of Ms. Jones. Not all readers took it as good-naturedly as did Ms. Jones.

Such slipups can occur with alarming ease under deadline stress and may become even more difficult to catch in speeded-up electronic editing. Although some automated systems offer

programs to help catch common errors, no software can substitute for the world-wise, eagle-eyed line editors who understand the human consequences of one word or one letter versus
another.

Of course, not every slipup brings serious trouble. Most will
merely turn an editor's ears Campari red. Readers of news
media tolerate a reasonable number of goofs and misprints,
relying on correction notices to set the record straight. For
textbooks, scholarly publications, reference works, and similar
enterprises, however, errata are as mortifying as holes in one's
tuxedo and not easily overlooked.

More serious than such embarrassments are legal troubles
arising from errors, offensive statements, or other material
damaging to someone's reputation, privacy, or morality. Publishers shift most of these troubles to their authors by including
indemnity clauses in standard contracts. The publishers claim
that since authors are responsible for the accuracy and honesty
of their texts, authors must also be liable for breaches of this
responsibility. The authors don't like it. They counter that no
individual can track all the potential troubles in a long manuscript, and that only publishers can afford fat policies against
legal damages. In early 1982, a few publishers began providing
authors with liability coverage under the publishers' policies,
but authors would still risk certain deductible losses.

However the risks may be divided, no reputable publisher is
eager to be sued. Publishing is a narrow-margin business.
Litigation costs the earth. "Justice" is excruciatingly slow and
unsatisfying. Legal insurance carries large deductibles and may
encourage suits. Indemnity agreements with outside authors do
not protect staff-written material, staff revision of an author's
text, or editorial art. Obscenity judgments inhibit distribution
and sales. Plagiarisms, hoaxes, and copyright infringements
that come to court reflect badly on the publisher, even if the
author is held responsible.

So it is that publishers smile upon staff who can sniff out legal trouble. The following comments are meant to put beginning editors on the right scent.

The Elements of Libel

Libel actions fall like rain upon the major publishers. When a new general counsel joined Bantam Books in 1977, some two dozen law suits were pending against that one firm, most of them alleging libel.* Major works with references to identifiable people often get a prepublication "libel reading" by legal experts. But a great deal of run-of-the-mill text will never reach such experts unless an editor is discerning enough to spot potential trouble.

How much libel law must editors know? Enough, at least, to recognize the major signs of danger. Most of us already have a gut feeling for the principles of libel law. We know that society's right to the truth must be balanced by a concern for individual rights, for the harm an individual suffers through a damaged reputation. But how much concern is enough? Too much leads to a "chilling effect" under which editors fear any utterance that might give offense; too little leads to recklessness and consequent injury to undeserving members of society. Gut feelings don't always make for fine distinctions.

So it seems worthwhile for editors to know how the laws generally define libel, some of the terminology used in libel cases, and where the lines are drawn between freedom of the press and individual rights.

Of course, each decision on whether or not to publish potentially libelous material must be worked out in its own environment. The ethical questions editors face in handling such material are not always resolved by legal definitions, opinions

*Heather Grant Florence, "Libel Law 1980: A Map of Tricky Territory," *Publishers Weekly*, March 28, 1980. pp. 20 ff.

coming out of "landmark" libel cases, or the simplistic "tests" offered in certain guides. For example, you might find you could get away with publishing a defamatory falsehood because the victim is a public figure and will not be able to satisfy the tough legal standard necessary to establish liability. One hopes, however, that no editor would sink so low, even to attack the most universally despised public figure. Editors are morally bound—if not always legally required—to take every precaution imaginable in verifying facts to assure that truth is being served when any member of society is being publicly kicked in the pants.

In my view, editors should answer three questions in the affirmative before publishing defamatory material: (1) Is it legal? (2) Is it morally responsible journalism? and (3) Would something worthwhile be lost if the offensiveness of the material were neutralized? From a strictly legal view, there are these questions to consider: Is it defamatory? If so, is it false? If false, and the defense of truth cannot be used, is it otherwise defensible?

The legal questions are many-faceted, to say the least. Libel law is a slippery, complicated area to begin with; it varies from state to state, and every Supreme Court libel decision seems to add a new phrase or twist for lawyers to ponder. The miniglossary below, read in the order presented, is designed only to help the editorial troubleshooter understand the basic rules of the game as it has been played to date in the courts. The definitions and discussions are paraphrased from several good sources (listed at the end of this chapter), but they are far from perfect as legal text. They are designed to get your feet wet, not drown you in detail.

Libel: A Miniglossary and Guide

DEFAMATION   An act of communication that causes someone to be shamed, ridiculed, held in contempt, or lowered in the estimation of the community, or to lose employment status or earnings or otherwise suffer a damaged reputation. Such defamation is couched in *defamatory language*.* Defamation of small groups can, under certain conditions, give claims to individual members of the groups. Corporations can bring claims for defamation.

LIBEL   Published material—text, headlines, photos, drawings, or any other representation—meeting three conditions: (1) the material is **defamatory** either on its face or indirectly; (2) the defamatory statement is about someone who is **identifiable** to one or more persons; and (3) the material must be distributed to someone other than the offended party; i.e., published.

Libel is a tort (an injurious, wrongful act) for which the offended party can seek **damages** except under conditions defined by state law. (*See* **Defenses**.)

IDENTIFIABILITY   To prosecute a libel action, an offended party must be **defamed** *and* **identifiable** through the published material. A good name cannot be sullied if it is neither revealed nor hinted at. But invented detail, by coincidence, might seem to hint at a real identity. Editors will do their best to assure that a character not meant to be identified is indeed unidentifiable. It's not always easy. Ever since a California therapist sued successfully because a novel's character seemed to be based—identifiably—on him, editors have been advised to grill even fiction writers about the background for their manuscripts. If necessary, the authors are asked to cloud the real settings, characters, and other elements so that not one reader can identify them with certainty.

SLANDER   Spoken, as opposed to written, defamation. A nasty slur in a speech, a shouted insult at a White House

---

*Words in italics are defined in the immediate context. Those in bold are defined elsewhere.

reception. Editors who deride one of their troublesome authors in public could be inviting a slander suit. Slander and libel are similarly judged and remedied.

DAMAGES   Those who cannot establish a **complete defense** against a libel suit can be made to pay the plaintiff special, general, and punitive damages—one type or more—the amount usually determined by a jury. *Special damages* are awarded to reimburse specific pecuniary loss suffered as a result of defamation; for example, loss from a boycotted business or from being fired. *General damages* are awarded to offset the presumed and demonstrated injury to personal reputation and the related mental and physical pain. *Punitive damages* are given to punish the offender and set an example to deter others. Sometimes damages go into the millions of dollars. The plaintiff, however, must prove **actual malice** (knowledge of falsity or reckless disregard for the truth) to receive punitive damages.

In most cases a plaintiff must prove special damages in order to recover. Proof of special damages is not required in cases where, on the face of it, the libel is obvious (*libel per se*), or where the statements, explicit or inferential, allege that the plaintiff (1) is dishonest or lacks the basic skill to practice his or her business or profession; (2) is presently suffering from venereal disease or leprosy; (3) is or was guilty of a criminal offense involving moral turpitude; (4) is an unchaste woman; or (5) is homosexual. False statements in these categories are generally presumed to cause injury to the plaintiffs.

ACTUAL MALICE   Publication of defamatory material "with knowledge that it was false or with reckless disregard of whether it was false or not." The term originated in a landmark 1964 Supreme Court case in which *The New York Times*, as defendant, prevailed over an Alabama public-affairs commissioner. The court ruled that **public officials** could not recover damages from defamatory material unless they established that it was published with actual malice. The *Times-Sullivan*, or actual-malice, argument has been applied to public figures as well as officials, but a 1974 Supreme Court decision (*Gertz* vs. *Welch*) in effect narrowed the definition of "public figure."

Actual malice should not be confused with *legal* or *common law malice*, which connotes ill will, spite, etc.

PUBLIC OFFICIALS People who work in a governmental capacity. Such public servants, the courts have ruled, must be open to "uninhibited"—sometimes even "caustic" and "vehement"—criticism in matters related to their official duties. Therefore, a public official cannot recover **damages** from defamatory statements without proving the defendant's **actual malice**. The press is thus encouraged to report robustly on government without fear of expensive suits; and, since almost any aspect of officials' lives can touch upon the performance of their public duties, the protected area is broad.

PUBLIC FIGURES Nongovernmental people who are of general interest to the public. As with **public officials**, the courts have allowed the press to cover their newsy lives without fear of **damages** from inadvertent errors. Since 1964, false statements about public figures have been protected from libel damages if published without **actual malice**. The courts may classify a plaintiff as a *general-purpose public figure*, of interest to the public in all aspects, or as a *limited-issue public figure*, of public interest only in certain areas of their lives and not required to prove actual malice for libel outside those areas.

Editors must remember that those classified as private persons need not prove actual malice to win **general** and **special damages**. Showing some **fault** or **negligence** on the publisher's part may be enough.

NEGLIGENCE, or FAULT Terms used to describe a publisher's failure to observe normal standards of verification before publishing defamatory material. Since a Supreme Court decision in 1974 (*Gertz* vs. *Welch*), the states have been free to substitute standards of negligence or fault for the **actual malice** test in cases involving private persons—even if the statements about them are of interest to the public.

PRIVILEGE, ABSOLUTE   An absolute immunity from defamation actions enjoyed by the President of the United States, members of Congress, Supreme Court justices, state governors, legislators, judges, and other high government officials in the performance of their official duties. Absolute privilege also extends to statements by judges, jurors, parties, lawyers, and witnesses in the course of trial proceedings and closely related contexts, such as settlements. The statements must be pertinent to the case. Those with absolute privilege may go on record with any defamatory remark, malicious or not, true or false, without fear of libel actions. In reporting these remarks, the press has only a **qualified privilege** (see below). Absolute privilege extends to a few other special circumstances, such as communications between spouses.

PRIVILEGE, QUALIFIED   While **absolute privilege** is based on the character of the speaker, qualified privileges are based on the relationship between the speaker and the recipient of the communication. Thus, a statement in defense of a defamation, a report on an employee, credit reports, communications between members of a group or a family, stockholders' criticisms of management, and criticism of public employees are qualifiedly privileged. Qualified privilege is available only if the communication is made without **common-law malice**.

There is also the *"reporter's privilege,"* which protects reports of official meetings, actions, or proceedings. To qualify for the privilege, the report must be fair, balanced, and impartial, made in good faith and based on the records—not on a one-sided selection from them. If one trial witness calls a defendant "insane" and the next describes him as "supremely well adjusted," a report citing only the former testimony probably would not be privileged against libel damages.

Qualified privilege also applies to documents entered officially into public records. In some states, documents filed for a case may be reported on as soon as they are submitted to the court.

DEFENSES   Certain circumstances, when proved in court to have framed an act of libel, cause damages to be denied or reduced. A defendant may plead one or more of these circumstances as "defenses" in libel proceedings. Those under which no damages may be recovered are called *complete defenses*; those that mitigate damages are *partial defenses* (sometimes called simply *mitigating factors*).

Complete defenses are of two types: an *absolute defense* holds up (renders the defendant immune from damages) even if **actual malice** is proved; a *qualified defense* does not.

Wise editors never publish defamatory material unless the defenses are clear enough to discourage most attorneys from instigating actions.

TRUTH   If the truth of defamatory material can be proved before a jury, it is an **absolute defense** against libel **damages**; i.e., no damages can be awarded, and **actual malice** is not an issue. But if truth is the surest defense, it can also be one of the most expensive, time-consuming, and unobtainable. When truth can be established only with a slew of records, affidavits, and witnesses, it will be worth considering other possible defenses.

CONSENT   Another **absolute defense** is proof that the claimant gave the defendant permission to publish the defamatory material. The best proof of consent is to have it in writing, with a signature.

FAIR COMMENT AND CRITICISM (OPINION)   So as not to inhibit critical, opinionated discourse on matters of public interest, the courts have protected what is called "fair comment and criticism" against libel **damages**; but certain criteria must be met for this **complete defense**: The material in question must be an evaluation, an appraisal, an opinion, not a statement of fact; the facts on which the opinion is based, however, must be stated. The opinion must be expressed without malice (common-law malice; i.e., spite, ill will), and it must not ascribe sordid or corrupt motives. Otherwise, the criticism may be as nasty and devastating as the publisher believes is justified.

MITIGATING FACTORS   (Sometimes called *secondary* or *partial defenses*.) Tactics and arguments used to minimize the effects a libel suit. At best, these defenses can get a case settled out of court, perhaps dismissed on pretrial summary judgment motions, with no **general** or **punitive damages** awarded to the plaintiff. Among the mitigating factors are: partial truth, lack of malice, **retraction**, and publication as a result of provocation. Some are discussed below.

REPLY OR SELF-DEFENSE   Those who are publicly attacked have a **qualified privilege** to fight back, provided the retort is free from irrelevant matters (does not go beyond the issues that provoked it) and was not known or believed to be false. Libelous remarks qualifying as reply or self-defense can be a **mitigating** argument or a **complete defense** against libel **damages**, depending on the circumstances.

RETRACTION AND APOLOGY   Current libel law is premised on the notion that some published error is inevitable, especially under deadline pressure, and that honest error must be defensible if a free press—which benefits society—is to be maintained. This premise is reflected throughout the law and in the consideration given to a published correction as a **mitigating factor**. Depending on the state law and graciousness of the injured party, a published admission of wrongdoing may reduce most of the **damages**—and in some cases completely satisfy the plaintiff in an out-of-court **settlement**.

A publication need not always flagellate itself to work out a retraction agreement. Though the urge to apologize is a noble instinct, lawyers warn that a hasty, superfluous, or ill-worded apology can jeopardize the defendant's case. Such a retraction could be a premature admission of guilt, a compounding of the original sin, or a compromise of legitimate defenses.

PROOF OF PREVIOUS BAD REPUTATION   A **mitigating factor** to reduce **damages**. It is difficult to tarnish an already tarnished character, goes this argument, which can be applied more easily to infamous villains than to those whose reputations may yet be saved.

SETTLEMENT, or ACCORD AND SATISFACTION   After a libel has been committed, a defendant may be able to wipe out the tort by negotiating an out-of-court settlement with the plaintiff. Such negotiations should be recorded in writing, with points of agreement signed, even if no money is involved.

Invasion of Privacy

And just when you thought it was safe to publish an unassailable truth, along comes invasion of privacy, which is an individual's right to be left alone and not subjected to undesired, undeserved publicity, even if it is true. Many an accurate statement or harmless-looking photo can invade someone's dearly cherished privacy. And that someone can make heaps of trouble for a publisher and editor.

Statutes and rulings have developed in most states to protect this right, extending it to all living persons except those who are of *current news interest to the public*—i.e., "public figures." Invasion of privacy differs from libel in two essential ways: First, the "injury" is to someone's seclusion and personal *feelings*, not, as in libel, to someone's *reputation* in the eyes of a third party. Second, because true as well as false publicity can disturb someone's privacy, truth is not a defense in invasion-of-privacy actions (except in "false-light" invasions, defined below). The key defense is legitimate newsworthiness.

Here are two good statements on what constitutes actionable invasion:

The essence of [invasion of privacy] . . . will be found in crudity, in ruthless exploitation of the woes or other personal affairs of private individuals who have done nothing noteworthy and have not by design or misadventure been involved in an event which tosses them into an arena subject to public gaze.*
[Invasion of privacy is also] no-holds-barred rummaging by the media through the private lives of persons engaged in activities of public interest, under the pretense of elucidating that activity or the person's participation in it.**

Would we high-minded editors ever associate ourselves with such heartless crudity and sordid rummaging? Certainly not, if we could only recognize it whenever we see it. Unfortunately, litigation gives rise to some very subjective tests for newsworthiness and "public-figure" status. And public figures may have a few areas of privacy still separate from the newsy aspects of their lives and thus inviolable.

Even the beginning troubleshooter, however, can recognize certain common types of privacy invasion. Most trouble comes from people's names or pictorial likenesses being used, without their permission, to sell something other than news. This type of violation is called *commercial misappropriation*, and is more likely to occur in *promoting* your editorial product than in preparing it. Even authors have been known to make trouble over the use of their portraits to sell their works. Most book contracts now calls for the author's blanket permission to use name and portrait in advertising.

Celebrities enjoy a special right not to be exploited in non-news contexts unless they get paid for it. Called a *right of*

---

*Paul Ashley of the Washington Bar Association quoted in "The Dangers of Libel: A Summary for Newsmen by the Associated Press," New York, AP, 1964 (booklet).
**From a 1976 California federal district court opinion, *Virgil* vs. *Time Inc.*

publicity, it is based on the property value of a famous person's name, face, and personality.

In general, you will *not* end up paying damages for using a photo of someone, without their permission, for communications on matters of legitimate public interest, including educational material and other nonfiction—unless the context places the subject in a false light. Damages *are* recoverable for the unauthorized use of the photo for purposes of advertising or trade.

As to use of a photo to illustrate fiction, the law is not clear. Certainly an editor would be ill-advised to use an unauthorized portrait as a cover illustration or in another prominent manner, even if the work of fiction portrays a saintly Nebraska pioneer who raises eight children to be senators and surgeons.

Can an editor use photos from a publication to advertise that publication? Yes. No damages may be recovered for use of news pictures (or other news items) to advertise the publication in which they first appeared—as long as such use does no more than present the content of the publication and does not imply the subject's endorsement. *Sports Illustrated*, for example, was allowed to lift a picture of football star Joe Namath from one of its issues and use it in a general subscription advertisement.

In addition to spotting commercial misappropriation, crack troubleshooters must recognize two further types of privacy invasion: public disclosure of private facts, and portrayal in a "false light." Both types can involve text as well as pictures.

Public disclosure of private facts. In most states it is a tort to publicize private facts about someone if those facts would be highly offensive to a reasonable person. Liability for such an invasion of privacy can, like libel, bring grotesque damages. But the press can still disclose whatever it digs up about anyone who is news or in the news. According to the statutes and court rulings of most states, disclosure of such "truthful and embarrassing private facts" is allowed when (1) the subject is a public figure; or (2) the subject is a nonpublic figure caught up in events or in a situation of general interest to the public. In short, when the disclosure is "news." (If the disclosure is false and defamatory, it is actionable as libel.)

Out of respect for the First Amendment, the courts have held the people's right to know about what interests them in higher regard than an individual's right to seclusion. The courts have recognized that what interests the general public might not always be on the highest philosophical plane. Still, several opinions have indicated that "newsworthiness" must be based on community mores.

"Newsworthiness," or "legitimate concern to the public," fails when a jury believes the private facts were published *solely* "for any inherent, morbid, sensational, or curiosity appeal they might have," as a 1976 opinion put it.

An invasion of privacy called *false light* is considered by at least one publisher's counsel to be the claim of greatest concern to writers. To show someone in a false light is to misuse or invent information about them so that the truth is distorted, even if the distortion is complimentary.

To defend against claims of false light, one must prove the truth of the information as it is presented or, in cases where a matter of legitimate public interest is involved, the lack of actual malice (knowledge of falsity or reckless disregard for the truth). In one famous case, an article allegedly described a fictionalized play as the true story of a family. The family sued but did not recover damages because the article, though partly false, was judged to have been published without actual malice. In another notable case, a reporter wrote that a recent widow wore a "mask of non-expression" when he visited her. In truth, the widow had been away when the reporter called. The widow won her suit on the basis of falsity and actual malice in the reporting.

Troubleshooting for false-light invasion of privacy is a matter of trusting the writer's reputation for sticking to facts or laboriously questioning every fictionlike passage. It isn't easy, especially in the era of "New Journalism."

Journalism by False Light, Fabrication, and Hoax

"New Journalism" derives much of its charm from flirtation with false light, disclosure of private facts, and libel. Many writers in the past have risked these dangers in pursuit of truth or profit; but some New Journalists seem to embrace them as tools of the trade. The editor's job is to see that flights of "gonzo" journalism do not crash-land in court.

Former *Harper's* editor Lewis Lapham comments in a superb essay* that the techniques of New Journalism have "more in common with the making of documentary films than with the writing of novels. The writer seeks to make an image, not a work of art. He begins with an attitude of mind and a mass of random observations—notes on the weather; tones of voice; landscapes; fragments of conversation; bits and pieces of historical incident; descriptions of scene; impressions of character. . . . In order to impose a form on the chaos of his notes, the writer decides on a premise and a point of view. . . . Novelists and sociologists borrowed the form of the empirical sciences, dressing up their stories in the costumes of 'case histories,' forcing the narrative into whatever language would carry with it the impression of truth."

Lapham blames the contemporary media audience for the success of journalistic "spectacles and grand simplifications," for the audience defines happiness "as the state of being well and artfully deceived."

It was this environment, Lapham suggests, that enabled a *Washington Post* reporter in 1980 to carry impressionistic journalism to the point of fabrication. The story, mentioned in Chapter 4 as a casualty of deadline editing, concerned an eight-year-old heroin addict and won a 1981 Pulitzer Prize before it

---

*Lewis H. Lapham, "Gilding the News," *Harper's*, July 1981, pp. 31–39. Copyright © 1981 by Harper's Magazine. All rights reserved. Quoted by special permission.

was discovered to be an invention. Not only did this infamous hoax stimulate an $8.8 million lawsuit in 1981, but also a new wave of discussion on the relationships between facts and journalism, journalists and their editors, and editors and audience.

Lapham warns that people will forgive the mistakes and distortions of a medium if faith in its underlying honesty can be retained. "But once let them suspect that the difference between fact and fiction may be as random as a number drawn in a lottery, and their resentment will wreak an expensive vengeance."

About the same time as the *Post* fabrication, another few print and television hoaxes were uncovered. Media executives, fearing public outrage, lined up to reaffirm their basic integrity. Editors dusted off the old safeguards against bamboozlement. In a half-page *New York Times* article* on all the editorial fallout, Jonathan Friendly described how "some newspapers have issued formal guidelines for their staffs on such topics as identifying sources, the use of incomplete quotations or 'composite' characters, staged photographs and prize competitions. . . . Editors generally say that they intend to reduce the number of articles that are inherently less credible because the principal sources are not named."

If one enduring reform emerges from the Year of the Hoax, it is likely to be that editors will subject staff writing to the same scrutiny usually applied to outside contributions, especially those unsolicited. Most editors are tough on outsiders, demanding that they identify their sources for sensitive material as well as their motives for going after it. But the same editors have allowed staffers to protect confidential sources from nosy cops, judges, and bosses. In many cases, of course, the bond of secrecy between source and writer has helped to uncover critical truths that otherwise would never have been shared with the public. But the cloak of confidentiality also has enabled a host of second-rate journalists to invent or distort their secret

*Jonathan Friendly, "Disclosure of Two Fabricated Articles Causes Papers to Re-Examine Their Rules," *The New York Times*, May 25, 1981, p. A7.

"sources" in order to come up with as hot and trendy a tale as any produced by the ace New Journalist of the staff. At the 1981 conference of the Investigative Reporters and Editors, a speaker asked an audience of nearly a hundred journalists to raise their hands if they knew of faked stories other than that of the *Washington Post*. Seventeen hands went up.*

In the wake of these incidents, many publishers will be considering "reform" policies similar to one laid down in 1981 for the staff of a Florida newspaper:

A reporter must share with his or her editor the identity of any confidential source on which we are going to hang a story before we publish it. Once confidentiality is pledged to a source, the editor must share with the reporter the burden of trust which neither can betray, even if it means going to jail together rather than breaking the confidence.

The essence of the reform, then, will not be the jailing of more editors—which would please too many authors. It will be the editor's involvement in what used to get by as "blind attributions"—sources, subjects, and spokespeople who, un-identified, could so easily turn out to be nefarious liars, com-posite characters, and out-and-out fictions.

Knowing who the sources are and why they are saying what they are saying will make it much easier for the editorial troubleshooter to sniff out fabrications. For example, a story always smells fishy when all its elements cohere perfectly to the author's point of view. Now, by reviewing the sources, the editor has a chance to judge the likelihood and truth of such "for-tuitous" harmony.

Disclosure of the author's research may help editors deal with another type of headache: plagiarism. Writers allowed to obscure their sources tend to get sloppy about crediting bor-rowed text, even long verbatim passages. If the borrowed pas-

---

*"Other Reporters Admit Knowledge of Fake Stories," *Editor & Publisher*, July 11, 1981, p. 16.

sages are protected by copyright, the sloppiness is very serious indeed; it is infringement of someone's property rights. The publishing industry's renewed attention to sources is bound to rub off on a few would-be plagiarists, who will not so easily "forget" that they read a brilliant passage somewhere else before presenting it as their own. If the author does suffer this lapse of memory, there are two ways the troubleshooting editor can catch the plagiarism: by knowing the original text well enough to recognize the stolen portions, or by questioning those passages in the new text that differ suspiciously from the author's normal style. Both these means argue for close examination of manuscripts by at least two widely read editors.

Editors, authors, and the public have much to gain, then, if the editor shares the author's confidential sources without betraying them. As for anyone going to jail for withholding sources, let us hope it does not happen unjustly.

Obscenity and Pornography

With the utter unpredictability of the courts in obscenity cases, and with the inevitable swings of society into periods of moral fervor, how can editors avert trouble without becoming censors?

True censors do not judge offensive material within its context. Most have in mind a set of specific words and situations—those that offend them personally—which they hold to be obscene under any circumstances. Editors, however, treat dirty words or other "obscene" representations as devices of communication, and will judge them by their effectiveness in delivering a worthwhile message to a particular audience. This is what the courts have done, or tried to do, over the last half century.

A landmark decision of 1933 opened the doors for U.S. distribution of James Joyce's *Ulysses* and seemingly every other work of literary merit. In 1957, the Supreme Court's *Roth* decision in effect broadened "merit" to mean *any* "redeeming social importance," and called for judgment based on the "dominant theme" of a work, not isolated passages. But in 1973 the liberal trend was challenged by Supreme Court Justice Warren Burger in his *Miller* vs. *California* opinion. Burger ridiculed the social-importance defense in declaring that the Constitution does not protect "a 'live' performance of a man and a woman locked in a sexual embrace at high noon in Times Square . . . [merely] because they simultaneously engage in a valid political dialogue."

According to Burger's new guidelines, a work could be judged obscene and therefore outside the protection of the First Amendment if: (1) the average person, applying contemporary community standards, would find that the work, taken as a whole, appeals to the prurient interest; and (2) the work depicts or describes, in a patently offensive way, sexual conduct specifically defined by the applicable state law; and (3) the work, taken as a whole, lacks serious literary, artistic, political, or scientific value." Burger further held that "contemporary community standards" could not be articulated for all fifty states in a single formulation," i.e., that there was no fixed national standard by which to review decisions at the state level.

Miller and subsequent rulings, along with statutes, have encouraged thousands of local actions against vendors, distributors, and publishers. Schools and libraries have suffered harassment, censorship, and even book-burning. At the same time, oddly, many communities have come to accept that a need, demand, and place exist for uninhibited sexual expression, as long as such expression is not openly pandered to those who would be offended by it or to children.

Thus, hard-core "skin flicks" and illustrated sex magazines are now advertised with restraint, yet they are wildly, desperately explicit as they try to outdo one another. And bestsellers from major trade publishers—sold side by side with religious cards in the nation's retail outlets—reach levels of prurience equal to any under-the-counter porno of a few years ago.

Serious trouble for publishers and even editors has come mainly from "pandering"—not from publishing—naughty materials. In 1965 the Supreme Court sent Ralph Ginzburg to jail for the way he advertised his classy-but-sexy magazine *Eros* through the mails and in newspaper ads. He had sent millions of advertising circulars through the post office of Middle*sex* (get it?), New Jersey, to indiscriminately chosen addresses, and the enticing material offended many parents and others who said they preferred not to see it. In the court's majority opinion, Ginzburg was called guilty of "the sordid business of pandering — 'the business of purveying textual or graphic matter openly advertised to appeal to the erotic interest of . . . customers.' "

A decision known as *Redrup* in 1967 held that two trashy sex novels published by William Hamling of San Diego were not obscene and could be sold on Times Square. To some legal professionals and scholars, the decision suggested that equally "non-obscene" trash could now be sold anywhere if it were not pandered to the general public. Under that interpretation, Hamling might have also gotten away with a later venture: an illustrated version of the controversial, government-sponsored document, *Report of the Committee on Obscenity and Pornography* (1970). But his firm pandered the work in a mail brochure reproducing some of the book's hardest-core illustrations, and in 1974 the Supreme Court upheld Hamling's California-court sentence of a stay in prison and an $87,000 fine. His chief editor had been sentenced by the lower court to a three-year prison term in connection with the brochure.

In general, editors working for legitimate publishers will have to go far out of their way to land in jail. They needn't spend inordinate amounts of time measuring the "patent offensiveness" of a word in a manuscript against the standards of each community. That sort of agonizing may be left to the courts— where the "Casablanca" standard is just as likely to prevail as any. That standard was attributed facetiously to Supreme Court Justice Potter Stewart, who wrote of obscenity that "I know it when I see it." The press conjectured that whatever Stewart had seen during his navy service in Casablanca was the standard. Other wags have defined obscenity as whatever excites a judge.

It is more profitable for editors to concentrate on the tastes of their audience than on the boundaries of obscenity law. In most publishing and broadcasting situations, audience tastes are likely to be exceeded long before state or federal statutes are. And when tastes are offended, sales may plummet—a fate worse to many publishers than the obscenity conviction, incarceration, and solitary confinement of their highest paid editor.

Good editors, however, respect the tastes of their audience, and know that to lead people by the libido is often the least effective means of communicating. Nothing is more distracting to an intelligent readership, for example, than gratuitous raunchiness—unless the gratuitousness itself is the message, as in certain types of satire.

Editors should never feel they have betrayed freedom of speech by deleting profanity, scatology, or prurient sexual matter that gets in the way of the art, power, realism, truth, meaning, style, or satisfaction of a work. If convinced that such matter does contribute something, they must then weigh its value against the negative reactions, financial damages, and legal risks it may incur before they fight to the death for its right to be published and distributed.

A Cherished Freedom

The very fact that an editor enjoys the option to delete or retain troublesome materials reflects the freedom of speech that is still more or less enjoyed under the First Amendment of the U.S. Constitution. The amendment states that "Congress shall make no law . . . abridging the freedom of speech, or of the press. . . ."

In this chapter I have talked about neutralizing the excessive liberties taken by some authors; but nothing I have said suggests that editorial troubleshooters take aim at our precious guaranteed freedoms or embrace every new, would-be abridgment of free speech by the moral majorities, citizens for decency, reactionary justices, demagogic politicians, and special-interest pressure groups of every persuasion. The current challenges to a free press are serious and must be met seriously. But not hysterically. When the press acts irresponsibly and tramples on other freedoms in the name of free speech, society will move naturally toward repressing it. Only responsible behavior by our still relatively free press will clear the air again. We must be vigilant and unyielding in protecting First Amendment rights, but not paranoid in labeling every objection to our practices as gagging or censorship.

We need not be chilled by the law's uncertainty and edit in a framework of fear. Let us rather show a tender, loving care for humane truth—a care born of compassion for those we publish about and for. If we are locked up for that, it will have been worth the price.

General Sources

Among the sources providing general background information for this chapter are the following:

Associated Press. "The Dangers of Libel." New York, AP, 1964 (brochure).

Florence, Heather Grant. "Libel Law 1980: A Map of Tricky Territory." *Publishers Weekly*, March 28, 1980, pp. 20 ff.

Friendly, Jonathan. "Disclosure of Two Fabricated Articles Causes Papers to Re-Examine their Rules." *The New York Times*, May 25, 1981, p. A7.

Gibson, Martin L. *Editing in the Electronic Era.* Ames, Iowa State University Press, 1979.

Johnston, Harry M. III. "Publishing Law," *Handbook of Magazine Publishing*. New Canaan, Conn., *Folio: The Magazine for Magazine Management*, 1977, E1–E6.

"Lawyers Address Authors on Reducing Libel Risks." *Publishers Weekly*, May 8, 1981, pp. 162, 164.

Mogel, Leonard. *The Magazine: Everything You Need to Know to Make It in the Magazine Business.* Englewood Cliffs, N.J., Prentice-Hall, 1979.

Nelson, Jerome L. *Libel: A Basic Program for Beginning Journalists.* Ames, Iowa State University Press, 1974.

Phelps, Robert H., and Hamilton, E. Douglas. *Libel: Rights, Risks, Responsibilities*. New York, Macmillan, 1966.

Sack, Robert D. *Libel, Slander, and Related Problems*. New York, Practicing Law Institute, 1980.

Talese, Gay. *Thy Neighbor's Wife*. Garden City, N.Y., Doubleday, 1980.

U.S. Commission on Obscenity and Pornography. *The Report of the Commission on Obscenity and Pornography*. New York, Random House, 1970.

The Libel Defense Resource Center

Formed by some twenty media organizations and libel insurance companies, the center provides back-up information and research service to libel defendants. Address: 404 Park Ave. S., New York, NY 10016.

6

Information Retrieval for Editors

A MODERN APPROACH
TO RESEARCH AND REFERENCE

THE COMMUNICATIONS PROGNOSIS for the remainder of the twentieth century is information, information, and more information, coming at us faster, and in smaller, meaner packages. Each gram of the latest electronic memory devices can store one trillion bits, or about one hundred million typewritten pages—just what we need in our "in" boxes!

Technologists and librarians have developed ingenious new ways to survive this information fallout, but too many editors cling to old research habits or take the paths of least resistance. When it comes to output, editors are frenetically energetic; who can shut them off? For information input, however, they tend to rely on:

1. Their personal office bookshelves, sagging with student texts, inherited tomes, bargain books, subscriptions, and review copies, but rarely balanced and up-to-date.

2. The handiest colleagues, friends, and acquaintances who are thought to know something about the subject in question—

or, in a real pinch, the first "expert" who can be reached by phone.

3. The organization's library or the local public library, provided the editor does not have to go beyond the news morgue, card catalog, reference shelves, or standard indexes— or deal with the librarian for more than a few minutes.

These approaches are charmingly human and would be fine if they worked. Perhaps they did get the job done in a gentler age. But the world has gone data-mad. It is drowning in its jargon. The media are festering with language-abuse, inaccuracy, libel, and fabrication. We obviously need better information, and we need it faster than ever. How can we upgrade our approach to reference and research?

There are three steps: Finding out what information sources are available, learning how to use them, and making the effort to do so.

For the type of information needed to process words—grammar, usage, style, production, etc.—an upgraded approach isn't very complicated. At the end of this chapter I've listed and described some of the best information sources available for desk reference. Most of them are self-instructional, and it will take no more effort to use them than it does your present and possibly imperfect desk-reference collection.

No busy editor, however, can be expected to master the organization and quick retrieval of all the world's general information, now increasing, as they say, at an exponential rate. How does one find the experts or choose among the thousands of research sources on any complex issue?

This is where modern libraries and librarians come in—if editors will only put aside old attitudes and let them.

An Editor's Best Friend

You probably formed a negative attitude toward the library at about the age you discovered the opposite sex. Today your approach to both may be outmoded, but here we will focus on the library problem. Not that I will teach you advanced library research in these few pages, or even attempt to do so. You'd probably find it as soporific as you did the "library orientation" sessions of high school, college, and your present organization. Such sessions try to cram in so much that nothing is remembered save the location of the restrooms.

It has been said that the best library training is to spend time in a good library. I would add: Start with a healthy attitude about libraries and a research project that interests you. You'll learn the advanced sources and strategies as you go along.*

A good library attitude means abandoning three common misconceptions: that librarians are unapproachable; that libraries never seem to have what one needs; and that libraries are useless for up-to-the-minute information.

An Enlightened View

Why is it that editors will brave the wrath of megalomaniacs and Mafiosi before they'll walk up to a librarian and demand some help? The excuse that we were all traumatized at the children's desk by a shushing-old-spinster-with-brooch is too facile. More likely, editors are unaware of the dramatic changes in the library profession over the last few decades. From the scholarly guardians of the book that they might have been a century ago, librarians have evolved into information *zealots*. The joy of their workday is to fill an information need; the bane of their existence is a scarcity of people coming to them with such needs. Those who do come by are often pleasantly overwhelmed by the librarians' skills and service-oriented attitude.

Librarianship has become a high-tech profession—it was one of the first to apply computer technology to information storage and retrieval. Yet it still considers itself a missionary, "human"

---

*Once you get started, some of the dozens of published guides to library use will have more meaning. To find these guides, search the catalog under "Libraries—Handbooks, Manuals, Etc.," or browse the shelves where the most common call numbers (e.g., 028.7 in Dewey) direct you. A few selected titles are given at the end of this chapter.

service, devoted to preserving civilization and keeping the world in touch with the data it generates. The goal of the American Library Association, the nation's oldest and largest library group, is "to assure the delivery of user-oriented library and information service to all." Every year, at the ALA annual conference, thousands of members enhance their skills and renew their dedication to the cause—after berating one another for not delivering enough information, not considering every need of users, and not reaching all levels of society.

Within the Special Libraries Association, the second largest group, the Newspaper and Publishing divisions meet hundreds of hours each year, distribute newsletters, and create new research tools, all to improve services to reporters and editors. Imagine, two organizations devoted exclusively to your information needs, and you hesitate to ask for help!

Librarians serving the media are designing systems to support background research; verify facts; index, file, and retrieve stories; and distribute relevant new literature as it is acquired. The last service, known as "selective dissemination of information" (SDI), is something editors can request of most company librarians. The editor defines the subject—say, any new literature on UFOs—and the librarian goes after such material and routes it directly to the editor when it arrives.

A librarian, then, is a professional who is schooled, indoctrinated, and paid to help you gather information at any level, from any source. Many people have been discouraged in brief dealings at the circulation desks with clerks and other library assistants thought to be professional librarians. They are not, and it makes a big difference in what you can ask of them. Busy librarians appreciate your patience; but if they should balk at your courteous request for information, don't hesitate to remind them (or their supervisors) of their professional responsibilities.

In most cases, however, you will have to restrain the librarian from giving you more information than you need at once. (And don't fear to do so; they can take it.) Librarians have trouble holding back because they are fascinated by how much even a small library can uncork on practically any topic. With a well-chosen print collection and a terminal to search the on-line databases and bibliographic networks, a good librarian can find, borrow, or refer you to enough specific or general information on your topic to keep you going for years. Let's take one example to dramatize the theme and provide a useful model for your next library research project.

Life in the Big City

Suppose, as a project editor, you are drawing up plans for a multivolume reference series on the major American cities. You want to get a feel for the information sources available to help you outline the approach, advise the authors, edit the manuscripts, and assure currency as well as accuracy and depth. What can a good library do for you?

Here, in a concentrated dialogue, are some suggestions a modern library pro might come up with.

Librarian: First, are you familiar with our on-line union catalog for the public?

Editor: Don't count on it.

L: I'll be happy to help out. The video display terminals throughout the reference area have replaced our card catalogs. With simple "user-friendly" commands you can search the catalog's bibliographic database, which consists of all the holdings in our six-library regional system. You can search by author, title, or subject; the records displayed will contain most of the information found on the old catalog cards. Moreover, our records show circulation status for each item, so you'll know right away whether the material is available and where.

We use standard subject headings in the catalog, and we also have separate lists of these headings for you to browse through before you begin your search.

You've got a very broad research topic. You may want to approach it from many directions, or set up a progressive search strategy.

E: What strategy would you use?

L: I'd probably start with a general overview of American cities in the encyclopedias—especially *Americana*, which is strong in this area. Then I'd look over the latest city guidebooks in our collection, all the while picking up specific topics to investigate later. I'd search the library catalog first under "Cities and Towns—U.S." and "Cities and Towns—U.S.—Bibliography." I'd also look under the names of cities and their subheadings, as in "Detroit—Economic Conditions." I'd try headings beginning with "City," "Municipal," and "Urban." I'd get further references from some of the books these headings lead to.

When I'd gathered plenty of general and historical background from book sources, I'd turn to magazines and newspapers for descriptions of contemporary life and conditions, and to government documents and specialized reference sources for up-to-date factual information.

E: Slow down a little. How do I find which magazines cover cities?

L: Such periodical guides as *Ulrich's* will identify magazines by subject; for example, *Urban Life* and *Nation's Cities Weekly* under your topic. To find out what's *contained* in the library's magazines, however, you'll need to search various indexes.

E: Don't tell me—*Readers' Guide to Periodical Literature*.

L: Absolutely, under such headings as "Cities and Towns" and the names of the cities. But there are many other broad as well as specialized magazine indexes. Some are in printed form and some in microform. You might want to try *Periodical Literature on United States Cities*, *Public Affairs Information Service*, and the *Magazine Index*. We can also search some online indexes for you on our reference terminals.

E: That sounds fastest. Let's go.

L: Fast doesn't always mean useful. On-line searching can be very expensive, and usually you're better off exploiting the print and microform materials first, especially if you need just a few citations. Should you need long, comprehensive lists of journal articles on a narrow topic, an elusive piece of research you can't locate manually, or something so new it won't be indexed in print, then we could go to the on-line databases. Say, *The Information Bank* for a starter. We would search these bases using key terms, separately or combined. For example: "Chicago/ Questionable or Corrupt Activities/ Politics and Government/ Except Mayors/ 1978–Present." Or maybe "Los Angeles/ Organ Banks (Human)/ Illustrations"—never know when you might need one.

E: Let's hope I won't. What I will need is tons of factual data. Where do I get it—cheap?

L: Back in the print resources. Offhand, I'd suggest *County and City Data Book*, *Market Guide to 1,500 Cities*, *Rand McNally Commercial Atlas and Marketing Guide*, *Book of American Rankings*, city directories, telephone directories, our pamphlet files with chamber of commerce materials and other relevant clippings and booklets, and our indexed newspapers on microfilm.

Other approaches might include the *Encyclopedia of Geographic Information Sources*, *Statistical Abstract of the United States*, *American Statistics Index*, *Statistical Reference Index*, and such Census Bureau publications as the *Directory of Federal Statistics for Local Areas: A Guide to Sources*.

E: Are we almost finished? What else can a library possibly contain?

L: *Area Wage Surveys*; *Patterson's American Education*; *The Municipal Yearbook*; *Cost of Living Indicators: Price Report*; *Uniform Crime Reports for the United States*; the *Official Museum Directory*; *The Weather Almanac*; *The*—

E: I'll come back tomorrow!

And the librarian could still be going. We've mentioned a few dozen reference sources. If you were standing in the Library of Congress Main Reading Room, you'd be surrounded by some 17,500 reference titles, many hundreds pertaining to cities, not to mention the eighty million more items in that particular library.

And remember, librarians are as eager to handle the silly-sounding reference question as the grand research problem. No one will bark at you should you ask, "Who was the most famous dog in Kansas City?"

You get the picture. Misconceptions one and two, that librarians are unapproachable and libraries never have what one needs, are problems of perception—of library fear and loathing—and dumb to carry around in the Information Age.

Misconception three, that the library is useless for current information, is belied by the on-line databases such as I've mentioned and by print and microform reference tools whose currency has been much improved by computers.

The New York Times Index is available on-line, as is the text of the newspaper. The *Newsearch* on-line database each day updates its index to some four hundred news media. The *Magazine Index* and *Newspaper Index* offer subject analyses of "hot topics" as little as two weeks old. Government-documents librarians keep current on the endless outpouring of information from legislative, administrative, and judicial agencies with the help of complex finding aids, some of them on-line. Many libraries tie into news and financial wire services and subscribe to "insider" newsletters. They prepare their own up-to-date indexes to local or specialized media and compile lists of local experts. And if all that isn't enough, they will telephone or teleconference with other information specialists in reference networks.

Information Brokers

There's always the chance that you won't have access to a good library* or that your librarian is backed up on other

---

*Don't give up too easily. See if your regular library belongs to a system or network with resources you can use. Check the outside-user policies of the local academic libraries. Or use the reference-by-phone services offered by every large public library. Just call the one nearest you and work your way up to the state library and Library of Congress if necessary.

projects and can't handle your deadline needs at the moment. An alternative service available to those willing to pay is the information freelancer or the incorporated "information broker." Using their own reference sources and on-line terminals as well as the resources of local libraries, these commercial information specialists provide quick reference, in-depth research, document delivery, analytic reports, and many other services. They can be located through your local telephone company's Yellow Pages or such directories in your library as the *Information Industry Market Place* (Bowker).

The Office Reference Shelf

The more editors know about the full range of information services available to them, the bigger they can think when they plan ahead, and the better they can face the unpredictable. For recurring, workaday information needs, however, editors under the gun must still rely heavily on their personal collection of dog-eared reference volumes.

Below I present what I consider to be an ideal basic collection for editors in the '80s. Because so many of an editor's routine questions concern words, style, and production, I've weighted the list toward these aspects rather than general information. Many excellent resources are omitted for the obvious reason that only so much can fit on the desk, shelves, and windowsills of an editor's meager office. (Check with your bookseller or librarian for later editions than those listed here.)

For all editors

Bernstein, Theodore M. *The Careful Writer: A Modern Guide to English Usage.* New York, Atheneum, 1965. (Also in paperback.)
Alphabetically arranged advice from the man who shaped the modern voice of *The New York Times* and of many of the nation's most careful writers. More than 2,000 entries. *Dos, Don'ts & Maybes of English Usage* (New York, Times Books, 1977) is a later compilation of Bern-

stein's usage advice with only minor overlap. The complete usage shelf also would include *A Dictionary of Contemporary American Usage,* by Bergen and Cornelia Evans (New York, Random House, 1957) and latest editions of Wilson Follett, H.W. Fowler, and Eric Partridge.

Bernstein, Theodore M. *Miss Thistlebottom's Hobgoblins: The Careful Writer's Guide to the Taboos, Bugbears and Outmoded Rules of English Usage.* New York, Farrar, Straus, and Giroux, 1971. (Also in paperback.)

This classic and Rudolf Flesch's *The ABC of Style: A Guide to Plain English* (Harper & Row, 1964, paperback) will provide enough ammunition to shoot down most critics of a flexible editing style.

Chicago Manual of Style, The. 13th ed. Chicago, University of Chicago Press, 1982.

First published in 1906, the Chicago manual is the closest thing in America to a national style guide. It is a masterful guide as well to the technicalities of bookmaking, production, printing, and, in the 13th edition, electronic publishing.

Flesch, Rudolf. *A Deskbook of American Spelling & Style.* New York, Harper & Row paperback reprint of 1971 ed.

Brief comments on many troublesome words and phrases in dictionary form.

Jordan, Lewis, ed. *The New York Times Manual of Style and Usage.* New York, New York Times Books, 1976.

A good authority for resolving questions on proper names and other words, phrases, and abbreviations in the news. *The Washington Post Deskbook on Style* (New York, McGraw-Hill, 1978, paperback) has useful sections on the federal government, and newspaper law and ethics.

Mintz, Patricia Barnes. *Dictionary of Graphic Arts Terms: A Communication Tool for People Who Buy Type and Printing.* New York, Van Nostrand Reinhold, 1981.

Concise definitions of thousands of terms from the printing, typography, binding, publishing, papermaking, and design industries. Well illustrated, and abreast of the new technologies. Seven useful appendices.

Morris, William and Mary. *Harper Dictionary of Contemporary Usage.* 2nd ed. New York, Harper & Row, 1985.

My favorite of modern-usage guides. Though other guides cover more terms, the Morrises have a good sense of the peskiest usage problems. They offer their own outstanding expertise and frequently present the opinions of the dictionary's "distinguished consultants"—166 in all, including many writing celebrities.

Pocket Pal®: A Graphic Arts Production Handbook. 13th ed. New York, International Paper Co., 1983, paperback.

Nothing disappears faster in an editorial office than the little *Pocket*

Pal, which explains complicated print-production processes with magical clarity.

Roget, Peter Mark. *Roget's International Thesaurus*. 4th ed. New York, Crowell, 1977.

> Not in dictionary form, but grouped by concept, with an index for locating specific words. Editors must take care not to misuse this type of thesaurus, which inundates one with concept-related words, not all of them perfect synonyms. If this bounty is too great, it might be better to use a strictly alphabetical "discriminating" dictionary, such as the excellent *Webster's New Dictionary of Synonyms*. Rev. ed. (Springfield, Mass., Merriam, 1973).

Skillin, Marjorie E. *Words into Type*. 3rd ed. Englewood Cliffs, N.J., Prentice-Hall, 1974. Legal chapter updated to 1978.

> To set up shop on a desert island I would take along an unabridged dictionary and this classic, authoritative compendium of editing and production information. Main sections: Manuscript, Copy and Proof, Copy-Editing Style, Typographical Style, Grammar [master this concise section and you'll acquire the confidence you've long sought], Use of Words, Typography and Illustration, and a Glossary of Printing and Allied Terms. A 35-page index locates the thousands of editorial nuggets as you need them.

Strunk, William, Jr., and White, E. B. *The Elements of Style*. 3rd ed. New York, Macmillan, 1978. (Also in paperback.)

> You don't *refer* to this quintessential little book of grammar, usage, and writing tips; you re-read it, twice a year.

van Leunen, Mary-Claire. *A Handbook for Scholars*. New York, Knopf, 1978. (Also in paperback.)

> An alternative to traditional academic style-books. Provides a new, graceful method for footnoting, and modern advice on bibliography and manuscript preparation. Will serve editors well for handling mechanics of scholarly text, though it is not a comprehensive style guide, as is the Chicago *Manual of Style*.

Webster's Ninth New Collegiate Dictionary. 9th ed. Springfield, Mass., Merriam, 1983.

> Assuming the staff has access to *Webster's Third New International Dictionary, Unabridged* (Merriam, 1961, latest addenda © 1981), generally accepted as America's best, then for consistency's sake the desk dictionary for each editor should be the *Third's* offshoot, cited above. Important appendices in the © 1983 *New Collegiate* are biographical and geographical names, and foreign words and phrases not yet part of American English. Among other fine desk dictionaries are *The American Heritage Dictionary of the English Language*, with abundant commentary on usage, and the *Random House College Dictionary*.

Webster's New World Speller/Divider. Rev. ed. New York, Simon & Schuster, 1971.

> A hand-sized volume listing 33,000 words for quick consultation on spelling, accent, and syllable division.

Zinsser, William. *On Writing Well: An Informal Guide to Writing Nonfiction.* 2nd ed. New York, Harper & Row, 1980.

> Appealing advice from a greatly respected editor. Not a ready-reference work, but one to keep near for inspiration.

For book editors

Bowker Annual of Library and Book Trade Information, The. New York, Bowker, annual.

> The almanac of the book community, with statistics, survey articles, directories, and a good index referring back to recent volumes.

Curtis, Richard. *How to Be Your Own Literary Agent.* Boston, Houghton Mifflin, 1983.

> Actually, a primer on the politics of book contracts.

Lee, Marshall. *Bookmaking: The Illustrated Guide to Design/Production/Editing.* 2nd ed. New York, Bowker, 1979.

> A handsome, lucid text for reference or educational use, widely accepted as a standard work. Integrates the design, production, and editing functions into one mission: "To transmit the author's message to the reader in the best possible way." Excellent bibliography.

For magazine editors

Handbook of Magazine Publishing. 2nd ed. New Canaan, Conn., Folio: The Magazine for Magazine Management, 1983.

> A compilation of practical articles from *Folio*, the *Handbook* provides the widest range of magazine editing and management advice of any single collection.

General reference

Concise Columbia Encyclopedia, The. Judith S. Levy and Agnes Greenhall, eds. New York, Columbia University Press, 1983.

> Succeeds *The New Columbia Encyclopedia* (4th ed., 1975) as the most useful one-volume encyclopedia for an editor's desk reference. Though it covers only a third or so of the material in the 1975 volume, it is updated to 1982 and a bit easier to heft to one's side. Strong in biography and worldwide coverage, good maps. Avon publishes the paperback.

Sheehy, Eugene Paul. *Guide to Reference Books*. 10th ed. Chicago, American Library Association, 1986.

> The standard finding guide to all types of reference works, indexed by author, title, and broad subject, with excellent annotations. Most libraries have this volume on the public as well as professional shelves. Browse through its phenomenal range of sources to see if a copy might be worth a place on your own shelf. If you can use it as a key to your company or local library reference collections, you'll soon become the fastest fact-finding editor in town.

World Almanac and Book of Facts. New York, Newspaper Enterprise Association, annual.

> Well into its second century and still the champion for comprehensiveness and usefulness. Second choice: *Information Please Almanac, Atlas, and Yearbook*. New York, Viking Press, annual.

Federal government information

U.S. Congress. *Official Congressional Directory*. Washington, D.C., Government Printing Office, irregular.

> Contains biographical sketches of members of Congress, plus lists of committees, commissions, assistants, diplomats, international organizations, press galleries, and addresses on Capitol Hill. Also, congressional statistics, biographies of Supreme Court justices, and more. For biographies of past members of Congress, use the latest edition of the *Biographical Directory of the American Congress* (Washington, D.C., Government Printing Office).

United States Government Manual. Federal Register, Washington, D.C., Government Printing Office, annual.

> The official guide for keeping up with the structure and key personnel of federal departments, bureaus, offices, commissions, quasi-agencies, etc. For Interim updates, use the looseleaf *Federal Yellow Book* (Washington, D.C., Washington Monitor).

Other important sources, not for the desk collection but to get friendly with in the nearest library, are these: *Congressional Record* (Government Printing Office, daily while Congress is in session), containing the President's messages, congressional speeches and debates, votes, and added insertions, with indexes; *Federal Register* (Government Printing Office, five times weekly), with highlights of actions by federal agencies, all presidential proclamations and orders, new federal regulations, rules, hearings, etc., and indexes; *Monthly Catalog of United States Government Publications* (Government Printing Office, monthly), a continuing list of new publications from all branches of federal government, with indexes and ordering information; and the publication, indexing, and educational services of three ambitious firms (ask your librarian or write for catalogs): Washington Researchers, 2612 P St., N.W., Washington, DC 20007; Congressional Information Service, 4520 East-West Hwy., Bethesda, MD 20814; and The Washington Monitor, 1301 Pennsylvania Ave., N.W., Washington, DC 20004.

Noteworthy

Arth, Marvin, and Ashmore, Helen. *The Newsletter Editor's Desk Book.* 3rd ed., Parkway Press, Box 8158, Shawnee Mission, KS 66208, 1984.

Balkin, Richard, *A Writer's Guide to Book Publishing.* 2nd ed., New York, Hawthorn/Dutton, 1981.

> This well-received work is rich in facts, figures, and inside information for editors as well as writers.

Barnhart, Clarence and Robert, and Sol Steinmetz. *The Second Barnhart Dictionary of New English.* Bronxville, N.Y., Barnhart Books, 1980.

> New words heard widely, but not yet appearing in standard English dictionaries.

Britannica Book of English Usage. New York, Doubleday, 1980.

> A 655-page compendium of English-language history, grammar, usage, style, and related topics.

Crawford, Tad. *The Writer's Legal Guide.* New York, Hawthorn Books, 1978.

Dessauer, John P. *Book Publishing: What It Is, What It Does.* 2nd ed. New York, Bowker, 1981. Dessauer is one of the industry's best analysts.

Johnson, Edward D. *The Washington Square Press Handbook of Good English.* New York, Pocket Books/Washington Square Press, 1982.

Judd, Karen. *Copyediting: A Practical Guide.* Los Altos, Calif., William Kaufmann, 1982.

Literary Market Place. New York, Bowker, annual. A directory of publishers and allied firms, organizations, and individuals.

Times Atlas of the World, The. Comprehensive 6th ed. New York, Times Books, 1980.

> Too big for most editorial shelves, but certainly an atlas to have nearby.

Also outstanding, at about half the price, is Rand McNally's *New International Atlas,* 1980.

U.S. Book Publishing Yearbook and Directory. White Plains, N.Y., Knowledge Industry Publications, annual.

U.S. Government Printing Office. *Style Manual.* Rev. ed. Washington, D.C., Government Printing Office, 1984. The highly regarded style guide for government writers and editors, with sections on capitalization, compounding, and foreign languages, is useful to all editors.

Vogt, George L., and Jones, John B., eds. *Literary & Historical Editing.* Lawrence, University of Kansas Libraries, 1981. Specialized advice for those preparing richly annotated editions of literary and historical works.

Guides for library research

Barton, Mary N., and Bell, Marion V. *Reference Books: A Brief Guide.* 8th ed. Baltimore, Enoch Pratt Free Library, 1978.

Cook, Margaret G. *New Library Key.* 3rd ed. New York, H. W. Wilson, 1975.

Cottam, Keith, and Pelton, Robert. *Writer's Research Handbook: The Research Bible for Freelance Writers.* New York, A. S. Barnes, 1977.

Downs, Robert B., and Keller, Clara D. *How to Do Library Research.* 2nd ed. Urbana, University of Illinois Press, 1975.

Gates, Jean Key. *Guide to the Use of Books and Libraries.* 3rd ed. New York, McGraw-Hill, 1974.

Genthner, Frederick L., comp. *Guide to News and Information Sources for Journalists.* San Luis Obispo (Calif. 93407), El Corral Bookstore, 1981.

Gover, Harvey R. *Keys to Library Research on the Graduate Level: A Guide to Guides.* Washington, D.C., University Press of America, 1981.

7

An Editor's Introduction to Copyright

WITH FIFTEEN QUINTESSENTIAL Q'S AND A'S*

MANY NEW EDITORS, baffled by the intricacies of copyright, thank the Lord a rights-and-permissions editor is down the hall to deal with the nasty business. In general, they *should* be thankful, for in its entirety the Copyright Law is a jungle. There are sections—such as those governing properties in the entertainment industry—not to be entered without a safari of attorneys.

The sections pertaining to print publication of nondramatic literary works, however, are fairly straightforward and not beyond the grasp of the careful reader. Naturally, a legal expert ought to be part of any nonroutine business involving copyright: drawing up a new standard contract, negotiating for complicated subsidiary rights, proceeding in a dispute over

---

*Robert G. Sugarman, a member of the New York law firm of Weil, Gotshal & Manges specializing in intellectual property law, kindly reviewed this chapter. Its flaws, if any, are solely the author's responsibility. —A. P.

ownership, and so forth. But for carrying out the routine copyright business of a small publication or answering the most basic questions of authors, a little copyright knowledge is not—as some lawyers would have us believe—a dangerous thing for editors.

Who Wants Copyright?

In Chapter 2, I described three ways a publisher acquires copyright: by "authoring" a work; by commissioning a "work for hire" and registering it under the publisher's copyright; or by obtaining a written transfer of copyright. Now two questions arise: Why would a publisher *want* copyright ownership when licensing is available, and why would an author want to transfer this ownership rather than license certain limited rights?

Publishers usually want ownership when the property is likely to have value beyond its initial use. If, in looking over an unsolicited manuscript, the editors project that it can be serialized in a magazine, issued as a hardcover and paperback, and sold to Broadway, Hollywood, and television, the notion might come to mind of owning all those juicy proprietary morsels. Along with that notion, however, will come the question of risk: Should the publisher pay the author a modest sum for serial rights only, or an outlandish sum for transfer of copyright (and thereby all rights)? What if the material dies its first time out?

Some publishers routinely seek to acquire all rights without extraordinary investment. The standard contract of many magazines, for example, now calls for the author to sign over (transfer) the copyright as a condition of being published. In defense of this practice, the publishers ask: "Why should we devote editorial, production, and distribution energy and costs to something we don't own and that we lose as soon as we've published?" And the author, if big enough, replies, "Because I'm *telling* you to, Buster; take it or leave it." But the run-of-the-mill authors, who need to be published more than the magazine needs to publish them, generally surrender the copyright. In most cases, it wouldn't have earned them an extra penny, and, for the magazine, ownership ends up being only an operating convenience.

Authors, therefore, will transfer copyright rather than license certain rights because (1) they may be given no choice, or (2) the publisher may offer compensation that seems reasonable. On a small trade publication, "reasonable" may mean just a few more dollars. A scholarly journal may simply point out the opportunity for wider publication and thus greater prestige.

The author may also transfer copyright for no better reason than ignorance of the law. Conversely, an editor can blow a chance to secure valuable rights by not understanding their availability. Editors involved in complicated agreements will do well to study one of the many good guides to copyright for authors.* For new editors dealing primarily with routine, one-time-use agreements and wishing to appear knowledgeable at staff meetings, I have anticipated some basic questions that will come up and have provided practical answers.

Q's and A's

1. *What is copyright?*

Copyright provides the following exclusive rights to an original work of authorship: to reproduce it in copies, derive works from it, sell or rent it to the public, perform it or display it publicly, and—when you're tired of all that and need the money—the right to transfer ownership. There are certain important limitations on exclusive rights, but you get the general idea.

Copyright protects only the particular, tangible *expression* of ideas (of concepts, principles, facts, methods, etc.), not the ideas themselves.

---

*Such guides are listed under the heading "Copyright—U.S." in library catalogs and periodical indexes. Be sure the works pertain to the revised Copyright Law effective January 1, 1978.

2. What kinds of copyrighted material will an editor encounter?
Mostly literary, musical, dramatic, and pictorial works.

3. What law governs copyright?
Public Law 94–553 of the 94th Congress, October 19, 1976, revising Title 17 of the U.S. Code ("Copyrights") and taking effect as of January 1, 1978. Known as the General Revision of the Copyright Law, it superseded the Copyright Act of 1909 and its amendments (though the old law still governs certain works created before 1978). Revision took Congress some twenty-six years. To make it a perfect law will require that many centuries.

Circular R99 from the Copyright Office, Library of Congress, Washington, D.C. 20559, gives brief highlights of the new law and a little background on its development. Circular R1, "Copyright Basics," contains practical information. *General Guide to the Copyright Act of 1976* is a fourteen-chapter training text from the Copyright Office.

The Copyright Office offers a general information service on procedure, but does not give legal advice.

4. How long does copyright protection last?
The term of copyright used to be 28 years and one 28-year renewal. For works created after January 1, 1978, the new law provides a term lasting for the author's life plus 50 years. For "works made for hire" after January 1, 1978, the term is 75 years from publication or 100 years from creation, whichever is shorter. About 175 years, then, is the longest any new work is likely to be protected. For this term, a precocious author would have to copyright a work at age five, live another 125 years, and in death enjoy the protection of an additional 50 years. (For expirations of pre-1978 copyrights, see No. 11.)

Works excluded from copyright protection, of course, are in the "public domain" (up for grabs) from the day they first appear. The largest class of such works are publications "prepared by an officer or employee of the U.S. Government as part of that person's official duties."

5. *What is "fair use"?*

The new law specifically recognizes the principle of "fair use" as a limitation on the exclusive rights of copyright owners, and it offers guidelines for determining what that fair use is. Editors are sometimes offended by the library or classroom copying that goes on within the boundaries of fair use, but they must live with it.

Fair use also works *for* editors when they want to reproduce copyrighted material for such purposes as criticism, comment, and news reporting. The factors determining what is "fair" are given in Section 107 of the law. They are: (1) the purpose and character of the use, including whether such use is of a commercial nature or is for nonprofit educational purposes; (2) the nature of the copyrighted work; (3) the amount and substantiality of the portion used in relation to the copyrighted work as a whole; and (4) the effect of the use upon the potential market for or value of the copyrighted work.

The factors are intentionally general, allowing interested parties to work out specific guidelines to best balance the creator's right to compensation with society's need for art and knowledge. What the parties cannot work out themselves will be determined through test cases in the courts and periodic reviews by the Register of Copyrights and the Congress.

6. *When does copyright protection begin for a manuscript?*

When it is written. Copyright vests initially in the author or authors of a work. The new law protects an unpublished manuscript from the moment it has been fixed in tangible form. When the work is published, however, full protection requires a prominent notice of copyright on each copy, with these elements: © (or "Copyright" or "Copr."), name of copyright owner, and the year of first publication.

7. *What is copyright registration?*

Filling out the correct copyright application form and sending it to the Copyright Office, along with a registration fee and, usually, a "deposit" of one or more copies of the work being registered. Registration is not required to establish the copyright, but it is prerequisite to an infringement suit and certain types of remedies. It is generally good protection.

8. *Who owns a "work made for hire"?*

The owner of a publication owns the copyright to all work done by full-time staff in the course of their daily jobs and to outside work explicitly commissioned "for hire." If there is no such explicit agreement, and no explicit transfer of copyright, then only a limited right of use passes from outside author to publisher.

9. *How does a magazine register its copyright, and who owns the copyright to the individual contributions to the magazine?*

A magazine (or newspaper) registers its copyright for each issue by filling out Form SE from the Copyright Office and paying a fee. Ordinarily, the publisher is listed under "Name of Author."

Here is how the law distinguishes between the magazine's overall copyright and the individual copyrights of the contributors: "Copyright in each separate contribution to a collective work is distinct from copyright in the collective work as a whole, and vests initially in the author of the contribution. In the absence of an express transfer of the copyright or of any rights under it, the owner of copyright in the collective work is presumed to have acquired only the privilege of reproducing and distributing the contribution as part of that particular collective work, any revision of that collective work, and any collective work in the same series."

Under the old copyright law, the individuals in a collective work had to register their own copyright in advance or request a reversion of copyright after the magazine published under a collective copyright. Now authors automatically own the copyright to their contributions unless they transfer it by written agreement. For many editors, especially those on small publications, it makes life much simpler to refer all requests for reprint rights and other permissions directly to the author—i.e., the copyright holder—rather than have to act as broker.

10. *If I own the copyright to a manuscript, do I also own the physical manuscript in its original form?*

No. Ownership of copyright is distinct from ownership of "any material object in which the work is embodied." No matter how much you've paid for all exclusive rights to the confessions of an infamous assassin, he or his heirs still own the original manuscript pages and may sell them to the highest-bidding eccentric. By the same token, the purchaser of that physical manuscript buys none of your rights as copyright owner.

11. *How do I know what's in the "public domain," i.e., no longer copyrightable?*

No U.S. copyright granted before September 19, 1906, can still be in effect; all renewals and extensions will have expired under the old law. Works copyrighted between September 19, 1906, and December 31, 1977, were entitled to a 28-year protection, plus one 28-year renewal. Copyrights expiring and not renewed during that period are in the public domain. If the first term has carried them past December 31, 1977, the new law grants them a right to renew for 47 additional years from the year the first term ends. Works whose renewal carried them past December 31, 1977, get an automatic 19 years added to the original 28-year renewal term. Protection for both types, then, would end December 31 of the 75th year after the original copyright year.

For works copyrighted under the new law, see No. 4, above.

12. *How do I find out when a work was registered with the Copyright Office?*

Large libraries have sets of the *Catalog of Copyright Entries*, which you can search yourself. The Copyright Office will also search its records, for a fee. Circular R22 explains "How to Investigate the Copyright Status of a Work."

13. *What about international copyrights?*

Identifying the U.S. copyright can be tricky enough without having to worry about copyright protection from abroad. But one must sometimes worry. As a rule of thumb, see what copyright claims appear on the work itself. If there is a foreign copyright, it might be worth finding out if the nation in question and the United States practice reciprocal respect of one another's copyright. The U.S. Copyright Office can help.

14. *When we purchase the copyright to an item, should the document of transfer be recorded with the Copyright Office?*

Yes, if the item has significant value and potential for further earnings—or if the previous copyright owner is a shady character. The document should be recorded with the Register of Copyrights. There is a moderate fee and a simple procedure; the Copyright Office can advise you.

Rights transferred after December 31, 1977, may be subject to termination by authors or certain heirs after some 35–40 years. The details, should you ever need them, are in Sections 203 and 304(c) of the new law.

15. *How much should I worry about copyright when I'm making very minor use of very minor items? What's the worst that can happen for an infringement?*

A good question. Some editors suffer from chronic copyright paranoia. Ignoring public domain and their many rights under the "fair use" provisions of the copyright law, they seek formal licensing to quote anything from the Bible to the U.S. Constitution. This excessiveness does nothing but hold up production. Most new editors, however, err on the other side. Those raised in a permissive environment have a tendency to take without asking. They reason, "Who's ever going to notice, anyway?" Maybe no one—especially among the readership of small publications. But if a copyright holder does happen to notice, take offense, and sue, it could cost the infringer tens of thousands in damages, legal costs, impounded copies, and other remedies.

I would advise new editors to take a cautious approach to copyright until they get a feel for fair use and ethical practice within their field. In the music business, for example, people are considerably more protective and vindictive than they might be in the world of scholarly communications—although one can always be surprised.

The entire General Revision of the Copyright Law is only about sixty pamphlet-sized pages, and almost every public library will have several useful guides to it.* A practical grasp of the main provisions can be acquired in two or three hours of study; it is worth it. And remember this: In the course of their careers, many editors become copyright holders themselves.

---

*Law libraries will have more technical works, such as Alan Latman's *The Copyright Law: Howell's Copyright Law Revised and the 1976 Act.* 5th ed., rev. Washington, D.C., Bureau of National Affairs, 1978.

The Book Editor

ENTREPRENEUR IN A MAD MARKETPLACE

What is a book editor?
Take a deep breath:

> A book editor is a woman or a man
> (let's say a she) with an eclectic education
> > & a summer's training
> (à la Radcliffe's Publishing Procedures Course)
> > & perhaps an MBA degree
> all of which she will put to use in
> estimating the cost and profit-potential
> of a proposed acquisition or in-house project
> & rejecting the idea
> > or supporting it & selling it
> to the marketing department
> & working out a contract with author
> > or agent
> > or packager

for each of 10 to 20 manuscripts a year
and parenting each project through the
5-to-9-month period of gestation into hard
              and maybe soft
                    editions of a book
which means
watching out for Baby's interests
in the struggle for a share of promo & publicity
                sales & advertising
while
she helps initiate subsidiary rights activities
with magazines & book clubs
& mass-market paperback publishers
& motion picture & television producers
& foreign publishers
                & all this between
weekly crisis meetings
& biweekly editorial meetings
& monthly meetings to transmit manuscripts
        to the copyediting & production departments
& quarterly conventions of one association or another
& all too soon the semiannual sales conferences
& annual trade show of the
        American Booksellers Association
& 100s of sessions with authors
              & agents
              & freelancers
& in-house staff who copyedit
& write catalog & jacket copy
& design & illustrate & do whatever the editor doesn't
            so
she can sneak in a moment at home
to do what most people think
           she mainly does
namely, read new manuscripts that a first reader liked
& edit substantively the accepted manuscripts

so the line-by-line editing & production & marketing
        can begin
   &&
who does all of the above & more
for the pay of a plumber's
apprentice
if she is one of
        the lucky ones.

If you're already a book editor, you'll have appreciated this many-faceted wonder that is you, but will never have had time to reflect on it. Perhaps now is the moment. Those of you who are not yet book editors—and just about every editor seems to get involved with books eventually—can begin your orientation here and follow it with four very solid works: John Tebbel's *A History of Book Publishing in the United States. Vol. 4. The Great Change, 1940–1980* (New York, Bowker, 1981), and these three, cited fully in Chapter 6: Richard Balkin's *Writer's Guide to Book Publishing*, Marshall Lee's *Bookmaking*, and John Dessauer's *Book Publishing*.

A Special Breed

Book editors have much in common with their colleagues in other print media. Newspaper and magazine editors could certainly produce their own breathy, free-verse monologues on the many jobs they do under murderous pressure for puny rewards. But book editing has a certain entrepreneurial aspect that is unique. With each monographic title, the book editor deals with a self-contained economic venture—a singular, detached consumer product that lives or dies on its own merits.

An editor launching ten titles a year is like someone opening ten different kinds of shops in that period and hoping to make a bottom-line profit despite the hideous start-up costs and obstacles to becoming well known, finding customers, and delivering the goods.

Editors in other media rarely face this entrepreneurial challenge, as much as they hope their work will help sell newspapers and magazines. Each article or issue they edit is only part of a collective enterprise and contributes in a relatively small way to its overall market performance. The individual contributions of a magazine or newspaper editor aren't measured by profit or loss. But book editors compile win-loss track records, and Big Brother is watching the percentages. Book editors acquire, not just money-making manuscripts, but market-rated authors to haul from house to house. They speak of being in a cultural *industry*. They edit to *sell*.

Book editors, mainly humanistic people, find their lives swarming with numbers—and to make matters worse, the numbers are some of the most discouraging in the business world.

Consider these rough but generally indicative figures, drawn from several trustworthy sources:

Book publishers in the United States: 12,000.

Americans considered regular book readers: 22 out of 100.

Books published yearly in the United States: 45,000 (new titles and new editions).

Books earning a pre-tax profit: 33 to 40 out of 100.

Median pre-tax profit for the book-publishing industry: $4 per $100 invested.

Annual book industry combined sales: $8.2 billion in 1980 (about one-third of IBM's sales for that year).

Probable earnings from a book selling, say, 4,845 copies @ $9.95 from a first printing of 6,000: None. Net loss of $3,500.

Retail bookstores worthy of the name: 9,000.

Average retail shelf life for a trade book: 6 months.

Books reviewed for the retail book consumer: 1 out of 10 published.

Unsold books retailer usually returns to the publisher: 25 out of 100 hardcover, 35 out of 100 mass-market paperbacks.

Mass-market paperbacks usually returned unsold from wholesaler: 50 out of 100.

Average orders resulting from direct-mail marketing: 1.5 to 2 out of 100 mailings.

Duration of editor's pep talk to traveling sales reps: 4 minutes per book.

Duration of sales rep's pitch to retailer: 2 minutes per book.

Escalation of average book price, 1975–1980: 39 percent.

Loss in library/institutional buying power, 1975–80: 6 percent.

Median price paid for mass-market rights to trade books: $4,000 to $7,500.

Going rate for movie/TV/drama options on a trade book: $500 to $2,500.

Movie/TV/drama options never exercised: 90 out of 100.

Why do publishers keep publishing in this mad market, and why do people fight to become book editors? For one thing, the madness is mitigated by some good numbers, particularly from subsidiary rights on hot properties and multiple printings of successful titles. Also, the madness can be tinged with joy—of action, high rolling, living on the edge. Publishing is a gamble and a sport; enough win big to make dreamers of the rest. Dollar sales doubled in the decade following 1972. Harold Robbins' books sell as many as 22,000 a *day*. Time, Inc., sold $425 million worth of books and recordings in 1979; William Jovanovich of Harcourt Brace Jovanovich earned $304,000 in salaries and bonuses, and Harold McGraw, Jr., $321,405 in 1979. (For most career editors, unfortunately, the dream ends at about one-tenth such top executive salaries.)

Why else do it? Because, however schlocky or arcane, a book is a more interesting product than a shoe—even if most Americans don't agree. Because, at its highest level, book editing is profoundly, intellectually stimulating. Because the product connects its editor to the power, durability—and sometimes the immortality—of the printed word. Because the profession carries some glamour and prestige. And because at the end of the book editor's rainbow is always the thought of the big bestseller or the backlist classic. Some even dream of the personal imprint—

An Arthur Plotnik Book
for Macdoublerow

—earned only by those few whom publishers will trust to deliver outstanding books on a profit-sharing basis.

The Varieties of a Species

Longtime publishing spokesperson Dan Lacy believes the very delight of book publishing is that "it remains an almost infinitely varied and complex, anarchic, constantly changing, unsystematic mess." He finds it growing more responsive to narrow, specialized demands as well as to mass-market trends. "The facile readiness to shape itself sedulously to the marketplace, which many think demeaning in publishing, is in fact its greatest virtue."*

The marvelous mess, the money madness, the glamour, the paradoxes, and the dreams together make the book-publishing community a very special and self-conscious one—some say incestuous, at least in New York. The publishing community people read about themselves in *Publishers Weekly*, talk about themselves in divisions of the Association of American Publishers, measure themselves in research of the Book Industry Study Group, and honor themselves—since no one else seems kind enough to do so—at the American Book Awards ceremonies. They have a few major goals in common—making money and making books that make a difference—and one chronic, universal problem: distribution, meaning a cost-effective system of delivering books to those who want them, when they want them.

For all that binds it together, however, the book-publishing community divides into all the usual castes and subgroups. Book editors alone come in hundreds of special varieties. They can be categorized first by the market they edit for: trade (the general public), religious, professional, book club, mail order, university press, elementary and secondary textbooks, college

*Dan Lacy, "Publishing Enters the Eighties," in *The State of the Book World*, Washington, D.C., Library of Congress Center for the Book, 1981.

textbooks, subscription reference, and others; then according to the submarket, say, juvenile trade books or medical professional books. Or the sub-submarket: young adult juvenile. Then, within each market, they divide according to function: procurement, or acquisitions ("belly"), editor; manuscript ("line" or "pencil") editor; copy editor; production or managing editor; then by rank: junior, senior, associate, editor-in-chief.

Book editors may further specialize by subject—cookbooks editor, arts and crafts editor—or by fiction and nonfiction, by hardcover or mass-market paperback format, by added-on responsibilities such as permissions or subsidiary rights, or by the profit/nonprofit, private/governmental status of the publisher.

An editor's job may cross through several of these categories or be partly defined by the unique nature of a publishing house (e.g., West Coast alternative feminist books). With so many possible combinations, mathematically there may be 4,835,927 kinds of editors. If only that many jobs were available! But there aren't, because most editors are asked to do a little of everything, especially in small houses employing just two or three full-timers on the editorial side.

Even in a good-sized trade division, an average editor might do some acquisition; much proposal evaluation and development; substantive editing; preparation of material for the design, production, and marketing people; some promotional writing; and volumes of correspondence with authors. In divisions such as children's or professional books, add to these tasks an endless amount of goodwill shoulder-rubbing with leaders in the market audience.

A Not-So-Gentle Rhythm

To many journalistic editors suffering through their daily or weekly deadlines, the stretched-out rhythms of book editing seem like life in leisure village. But over a year there is probably just as much ulcer-making deadline pressure in book editing as in news journalism.

John Farrar of Farrar, Straus & Giroux began his publishing career as a magazine editor. In an essay "Securing and Selecting the Manuscript,"* he compares the seasonal lists of book publishing to issues of a magazine. In a given span of time, the editor must see to it that the new list, like a new issue, is strong in each of its departments and has appealing variety, important writers, and balance; then the editor must coordinate all the details of getting the list out.

Into the editor's pressure cooker also go all the outside meetings and events tied to marketing and sales. Religious books must be ready in time for the meeting of the Christian Booksellers Association in the summer, if any energy remains after the earlier summer meetings of the American Booksellers Association, American Library Association, and Canadian Booksellers Association, to mention a few.

Elhi (elementary and high school) textbook materials must be ready for adoption-board evaluation a year before they will reach the classrooms. Calendars must be published some nine months before the year starts. Christmas items must be out by October at the latest. Books for the college market must be in the professors' hands by April for the coming fall term.

And on and on it goes, without relief. Yet, because of the relatively longer editing cycles, people still expect books to be more thorough, accurate, and enduring than other print media. The book industry usually lives up to these expectations in such areas as reference, where fastidious editing is the *sine qua non* of staying in business. In other areas, editorial care has become a low priority.

Time magazine cited some horrendous examples of shoddy work in "The Decline of Editing" (September 1, 1980). The book publishers and editors *Time* interviewed generally agreed that manuscript editing is in decline and gave reasons for it: The great line-by-line editors are now too busy to pay much attention to each book, and the new generation of copy editors is

---

*In *What Happens in Book Publishing*. 2nd ed., edited by Chandler B. Grannis. New York, Columbia University, 1967.

inadequately trained. Lists grow larger, deadlines shorter, staffs smaller. One editor notes that "books on tight schedules are proofread in hunks by different people, and in some cases copy editing is done the same way." The copy-editing cycle for an average trade book is a month. At times it has to be done in a week. "Instant" paperbacks tied to a current event are put together from concept to sales rack as fast as a fortnightly magazine.

Advocacy Within the Bounds of Solvency

It is easy to blame the deterioration of high editorial standards on those unloved, Johnny-come-lately proprietors of the publishing industry, the conglomerates, with their alleged "bottom-line" and "blockbuster" mentalities. But many argue that the business-wise conglomerate managers have been good for the general health of book publishing and that the range of material published, lowbrow to highbrow, is greater than ever.

Yet everyone will admit that author-editor relations are not what they supposedly were in the days of Maxwell Perkins. Warm and symbiotic author-editor friendships still exist; but to the average new author signing a contract, the editor is seen as the hard-nosed publisher's advocate, beating down advances on the basis of the most pessimistic estimates of sales versus costs. And true enough, at this point the editor is more concerned with the publisher's interests than the author's. Once the book is signed up, however, the editor will advocate its general importance and some of the author's special interests, giving the project a chance to compete for limited resources with other works in house. The editor, of course, stands to gain from any attention that can be won for her or his projects.

The best editors, then, advocate the sometimes conflicting interests of three parties: publisher, author, and consumer.

The publisher wants to remain solvent, and the editor who believes in getting paid will advocate nothing that compromises this basic principle. A money-losing book will be advocated, yes, but usually only for an author expected to make money for the house over the long run. Even university and other subsidized publishers are loathe to operate in the red.

Author advocacy is toughest when an editor goes out on a limb to take a marginal title. Somehow the editor must overcome apathy and even hostility to the book to get its writer a fair shake. Opposing sales-motivated ideas that would undermine an author's intentions can be a very lonely job indeed.

Lonelier still, perhaps, is the editor's role as consumer advocate. Sometimes the editor must fight both author and publisher to see that a book satisfies its ultimate judge, owner, and financier: the reader.

Only the editor, who has the reader's interests in mind when a project is accepted, can keep those interests from being forgotten as the project moves along. Reader advocacy is a form of quality control, a job for worriers. Who will worry about whether an author's facts are up to date? Whether the messages are clear? Whether the design is appropriate for the audience? Whether the jacket copy tells the truth? Whether the book can deliver what marketing has promised? Sometimes the author will worry. Sometimes the marketing and sales departments. But always the editor. The buck stops here, even if the book doesn't.

9

Art for Communication's Sake

A GUIDE TO EDITORIAL GRAPHICS

PERHAPS YOU ARE STRICTLY A PROOFREADER, copy editor, or assistant editor whose duties have nothing to do with communications graphics. Maybe the only picture in your whole publishing operation is on the boss's desk: a grandchild glaring ruby-eyed from its leather frame. It doesn't matter. Sooner or later in your editorial career you are going to run across graphics, or graphics will run across you, and your very well-being may hang upon your understanding of a term.

If ever it was, graphics is no longer the frosting on the editorial cake. In competition with television, the print media use graphics not only to complement the message of the printed word, but to herald that message, package it in digestible chunks, and deliver messages independent of the word.

What some consider a graphics revolution was sparked in the late 1960s by Milton Glaser and his associates, who designed *New York* magazine and brightened up several other publications. The style they made famous—heavy rules and bars, boxes, virile typefaces, wide-angle photography, and campy cartooning—soon spread to such previously staid magazines as the *Saturday Review*; to newspaper feature layouts, including whole sections of *The New York Times*; and to trade and professional journals.

It can be argued that the surge toward "supergraphics" is a cultural regression, a television-inspired flight from intellectual content to an infantile, picture-book mentality. But it cannot be argued here, where my aim is simply to help editors penetrate the mystique of graphics or understand the bad moods of their art directors.

On small publications, editors who can barely tape a snapshot into an album often find themselves doing sophisticated layouts. They may handle some of the routine camera work and use do-it-yourself kits for special lettering and other effects. For such editors it is easy to lose sight of the point of diminishing returns, because playing amateur art director is more fun than struggling with manuscripts or hacking out blurbs for back-of-the-book departments. I've seen too many $25,000-a-year editors stretching an hour's layout into a day's work just for the relaxation and creative joy of it. My advice: A moderate amount of graphics activity is healthy and broadening for all editors; but too much distracts from the tough, sometimes tedious work with words. Most of the graphics should be done by art staff or freelance art people—who have much less fun at it because they're expected to be fast and flawless.

A Crash Course in Graphics Terminology and Techniques

Below, I've listed some of the most common terms used by publication art directors and graphics **suppliers** (typesetters, keyliners, photo-processing labs, photoengravers, strippers, printers, etc.) and translated them into language as nontechnical as possible without lapsing into baby talk. Still, the concepts come thick and fast for the novice. Take them one at a time, stopping to picture what has been described, and it will pay off. Editors who can handle just these terms will begin to understand the graphics people they deal with—even those who practice technical mumbo jumbo to keep editors off their backs.

Art: Any illustrative or decorative material as opposed to the **body type**, which is the paragraph-by-paragraph text. When an editor writes "art to come" at the end of a manuscript or galley, it does not mean the Mona Lisa is on the way; the "art" can refer to something as ordinary as a fancy border.

Halftone: As commonly referred to in black-and-white printing, a halftone is art that looks like a photograph but on closer inspection lacks the unbroken or **continuous tones** of gray. Instead, the halftone consists entirely of small black dots of varying dimensions, or **density**. The sizes and spacing of the dots give the illusion of grays when seen from the reader's distance. In printing with one color—the black ink of the text— the only way to simulate the continuous gray tones of the original art is to break up those tones into a pattern of black dots on a white background. This breaking-up process, in which light from the original passes through screens of standard densities before it reaches the negative film, is called **screening**, discussed below in more detail. The finer the screen and the more dots, the smoother-looking the gray. Cheap, coarse paper calls for coarse screening, which is why pulp-newspaper halftones sometimes look like dirty footprints .

A normal halftone may appear to have pure white areas, but even the whitest areas of the original usually end up with a dot pattern in the halftone reproduction, visible under a magnifying glass. A **burned out** halftone, however, will have no dot in the brightest parts—the **highlights**—of the picture (see also "halftone dropout").

TIP: Murky halftones can result from over-inking, too absorbent a paper, too fine a screen for the paper, or too large a **shadow dot**. The shadow dots are the large, unconnected dots in the dark gray areas. If the dots run together, the result is black.

Line art or linecuts: Art created with solid tones only; there are no gray or other intermediate tones to be reproduced by screening. A black-and-white pen drawing, for example, is solid black ink on a white background; therefore, it may be reproduced directly, with the solid black ink of the printing press representing the original black areas. No dot patterns are necessary. The artist can produce shading effects, however, by various crosshatching or manual dotting techniques, as in fine etching. Other techniques, such as laying down a transparent, adhesive line screen, can create an illusion of continuous-tone gray, but usually not with the same "photographic" look of a halftone gray. Since no screening process is required, the preparation of line art for printing is usually a little cheaper than the making of halftones.

TIP: Be sure to specify "line" for preparation of art consisting of one solid tone on a blank background, such as ink drawings and cartoons, solid logos, and large display type (14-point and above); otherwise, the design may be shot halftone, making the blacks paler and creating an overall block of very light gray, since a normal halftone translates everything—even pure whites—into dot patterns.

Dot screen: A regular pattern of dots used to simulate a continuous tone in reproduction for printing. A continuous tone, such as the solid dark gray of an original photograph, is rephotographed through a special screen, creating a dense pattern of solid dots. A light gray or white through a screen produces a sparse pattern consisting of very small, or **pin dots**.

Screens are also used as overlays to emphasize an area on the printed page. Such a screen must be sparse enough to allow the material beneath it to show through. The illusion is that of an area tinted gray or another color. Screens used in this manner are called **tint blocks**.

Screens are measured in two ways: (1) by how many rows

("lines") of dots there are per inch, and (2) how large these dots are on each row. A screen for making a halftone is selected by the first measure; i.e., one chooses a screen ruled in so many lines per inch. The more lines, the better the detail, provided the lines don't run together when printed on an absorbent paper. Screens used in newspaper halftones are usually in the range of 65–100 lines per inch. Screens for fine-art printing on coated paper may be 150 and up.

When choosing a tint-block screen, one is concerned with the second measure—the size of the dots—because all the dots are the same size to provide a uniform tint. So one chooses the correct **percentage screen** for the desired overall lightness or darkness.

Putting the two measures together, then, suppose a magazine uses a 133-line screen for all its halftones and tint blocks. For the latter, it will need to specify percentage as well. If the dots of a 133-line screen cover 50 percent of their background, they constitute a 133-line, 50-percent screen—which would print medium to dark, depending on the color of ink. A 133-line, 10-percent, tint-block screen printed in black ink on white paper yields a light gray. A 20-percent screen printed red on white creates a deep pink effect.

TIP: Some **texture screens** are made up of wavy lines or other patterns to create special illusions, such as the look of a TV screen. Ask your art director or photoengraver which texture screens are available to you, and then forget about them. They usually junk up rather than strengthen your graphic design.

Moiré: Sometimes the only art available to go with a story is a halftone already printed in another publication. An attempt to shoot this once-screened reproduction through another halftone screen may result in an imperfect superimposition of the two dot patterns. This unwanted checkered effect is called moiré. It can often be corrected by the photoengraver, but now and then moiré has to be lived with.

Line conversion or high-contrast reproduction: The drama of pure black-and-white can be achieved when an original of varying gray tones is shot as line art instead of halftone. Dark grays will come out black, light grays white. The effects range from messy and incomprehensible to stark and forceful. Usually, uncluttered originals that were shot in strong light work best, but one is never certain until the linecut is made. A simple preview method is to run off a xerographic copy of the original photo; you'll see approximately which areas will pick up in black and which will drop out.

One note of caution: The high-contrast repro and its variations, like the peppery mezzotint, have been overused and are now rather tired graphic clichés. The drama to be achieved with them depends mainly on the intrinsic power of the artwork. Be selective and sparing.

Halftone dropout: To keep white areas of the original art pure white, and gray areas gray, one orders a halftone dropout from the photoengraver. (To **drop out** or **reverse out** means to make a graphic element "print" white on white paper. If lettering is dropped out, it ends up white in contrast to the inking around it.) Halftone dropouts are commonly used to reproduce drawings that contain black, white, and gray; for example, about half the drawings in *The New Yorker*. The gray areas of the original are screened and become a halftone gray; the black line of the original is also screened and becomes an almost-black halftone gray. The white, overexposed, drops out white.

TIP: Because photoengravers only estimate the amount of overexposure necessary to create each halftone dropout, the lightest grays of the original will sometimes drop out along with the white areas. One must be vigilant in checking proofs. Underexposed dropouts may need hand **opaquing** to eliminate unwanted tone.

Offset preparation: The process by which the type and graphics for a page are assembled and converted into a sheet of film representing the final layout. The prepared film goes to the platemaker (usually part of the printing plant), where it will be converted into the metal plates that wrap around the cylinders of an offset printing press.

A traditional "full-service" **prep house** will (1) set the type; (2) **keyline** it onto a page layout; (3) shoot the type and graphic elements on a copy camera at the sizes specified by the editor; (4) strip—i.e., cut and tape—these elements of film into pages according to layouts provided by the editor (see Stripper); and (5) convert each stripped-together page into a single piece of film. Modern computer systems can eliminate these steps, taking text and graphics from digital form to page layout to printing plate— neat and fast, but not cheap.

Stripper, stripping, and platemaking. A prep house **stripper,** who bears no resemblance to Gypsy Rose Lee, is to the offset printing process what the **compositor** was to the virtually extinct **letterpress** process. The compositor assembled blocks of metal type and metal picture plates into a page makeup. The stripper assembles pieces of film. Computer page assembly, however, has put the stripper on the list of endangered species.

Strippers who do their own camera work begin with these elements: the body type, which has been fixed in position on a page-layout sheet or board by **keyliners;** the original art, marked with instructions from the editors; and additional, "loose" elements, such as advertisements, standing department logos, tint blocks, fancy type, and other decorations not put in position by the keyliners. Using a **copy camera,** which reduces or enlarges by percentage settings, the strippers convert the original type, graphics, and loose elements into pieces of sturdy film. Then, following the editors' overall layout instructions, the strippers arrange the pieces of film in the correct relative positions. This step is performed on a spacious **light table,** upon which the strippers lay down a large sheet of orange paper called **goldenrod.** Then, using T-Squares, triangles, and razors, the strippers mark off the page areas, cut holes called **windows** in the goldenrod wherever a film image must show, and tape the film in position.

When a group of film pages has been assembled on the goldenrod sheet, the strippers make a paper proof of this group for editorial scrutiny. The editors will mark those revisions necessary to keep the finished product up to general standards, but not such arbitrary revisions as will require a great deal of reshooting and reassembly at this late stage in the production cycle. Some examples of instructions for necessary revisions might be these:

1. Repair broken rule.
2. Clean hickey (speck of dirt) on advertisement.
3. Caption is touching photo; open up a half-pica.
4. Tint block is too heavy; go to 10-percent screen.
5. Flop (invert) portrait—face should be looking to the right.

And some revisions possibly too arbitrary for last-minute consideration:

1. Replace half-point rules with one-point rules.
2. Tighten depth of page one-half pica to match opposite page.
3. All captions a half-pica too far from photos; close up.
4. Letter "g" is missing descender in first col., line 3; hold page for new type and substitute.
5. Don't like photo layout; switch pictures B and E; remove pictures F and G and blow up picture A to fill space. (TIP: The more clustered a layout, the more difficult for the stripper to tape down each picture without obscuring part of the next. Extra sheets of goldenrod and extra exposures may be required for each row of a tight layout. The initial time and cost of an elaborate layout is bad enough; extensive revision can be very ill-advised. Consult with your stripper.)

When all revisions have been made to the editor's satisfaction, the strippers group the goldenrod assemblages according to a production editor's **imposition** (arrangement of pages). These groups are called **forms**. The forms are converted into large, one-piece sheets of film for the platemaker.

The **platemaker** will burn these film impositions into light-sensitive metal plates. Now the formidably complex offset printing process gets underway. To appreciate it, beginning editors should seize the first opportunity to visit the printer's plant and watch their own publication run through the presses. They will see how each metal plate, wrapped around a cylinder (**plate cylinder**) picks up ink from a **fountain** and transfers a one-color image to a rubber cylinder (rubber **blanket** or **offset cylinder**), which in turn will roll the print image onto a **web** of paper squeezed against the rubber by an **impression cylinder**— all at astonishing speed.

Duotone: Only an Arizona sunset is prettier than a good duotone, which is one picture printed in two layers of halftone dots, each a different color, to produce a richly burnished effect and intensify detail. The photoengraving cost is about three times the normal halftone price, and a second-color run is required on press.

Second color can be added to a black halftone also by means of a tint block (see above). The even-patterned screen of the tint block, however, creates a flat, overall shade of color and diminishes detail.

A duotone of black and warm brown is perhaps the most common; it takes on a coppery burnish. Darker browns mixed with black yield a nice hardwood tone in the dark areas and a bluish cast in the highlights.

TIP: Photos with a good range of tones—dark, light, and plenty of medium—usually make the best duos, but certainly not in all colors. Some yellows, for example, can reproduce a perfectly nauseating duotone. With original art in hand, ask the advice of your preparation people or consult a handbook showing sample duotones for all the common printing colors.*

Imposition and press runs: Nothing imposes more on a new editor than having to deal with imposition—i.e., the arrangement of pages on the press—and the technology of offset print-

---

*One good aid: Harvey Sternbach, *Halftone Reproduction Guide*. Great Neck, N.Y., Halftone Reproduction Guide, ca. 1972. Distributed by Perfect Graphic Arts Supply, P.O. Box 62, Demarest, N.J. 07627.

ing. For most publications, groups of 4, 8, 16, or 32 pages are printed across large rolls (**webs**) of paper, front and back, as they run through a press. When these groups of printed pages, or **forms**, are cut off the rolls, folded into **signatures**, bound together, and trimmed at the edges, naturally the individual pages have to be in sequence. That's the easy part.

The difficult part is understanding the mechanics and economics of the press, so that second and third **matched colors** and **full-color art** will fall on pages that can accommodate them and be printed as cheaply as possible. For the cost of press time makes surgical fees look reasonable.

If necessary, imposition can be learned after a few months of dialogue with your printer and a study of the imposition diagrams the printer uses for arranging pages on the printing plates. Editors not involved in setting up a **print order**—the instructions to the printer—might still find the following concepts useful:

1. Different forms (groups of pages printed together) can have different deadlines. Ideally, all late-closing material should go on a single form so as not to cause expensive delays of others.

2. Putting the dot of one *i* in color costs the same on press as coloring every last speck of print on the page. Consider if you might not get by using black only, keeping color forms to a minimum.

3. Confining additional colors (i.e., additional to basic black) to one side of a sheet running through the press saves good money. The impositions indicate which pages are on "top" or "bottom" sides.

4. Printers offer many options on equipment to be used for your press runs. You can waste staggering amounts of money using "more press" than you need for a given number of pages and color requirements. No one prints a 56-page publication on three press forms of 32, 16, and 8 pages if the color and other imposition requirements can be worked out on two, a 32 and 24. And only a maniac or saboteur would order a one-color, eight-page form run on a press with a capacity for four colors

and 32 pages. In short, the idea is to take maximum advantage of the equipment being used for every form, unless the printer has agreed in writing to take the lumps for underuse.

Full-color reproduction: Full color usually means four color, because most ordinary hues can be produced by printing-press combinations of three **process inks**—yellow, blue (cyan), and red (magenta)—plus black ink to intensify detail. Some 1,450 distinct hues can be produced by three-color process, mixing varying strengths of yellow, blue, and red two at a time or all together. A good black, however, cannot be produced without a black ink added to the process.

Used well, full color adds enormous impact to a printed page. When *Time* and *Newsweek* went all out on quality color illustrations toward the end of the seventies, one wondered how anyone could have plowed through the drab black and gray pages of the preceding years. In more specialized magazines, color brings out detail, beauty, and dimensions never realized in black and white. Color pleases readers.

But color-printing has a language and an economy all its own, and, because it offers the amateur more chance to louse up and waste money than does any other editorial operation, it should be left whenever possible to the production experts. An editor may not have such experts handy, however, and may face an opportunity to use glorious color at a cost that should not be refused. For example, an advertiser wants a four-color page, which is usually priced high enough to support the cost of running a four-color press form. So, if a splash of editorial color can be prepared cheaply and put on one of the pages of that form, it makes sense to take the "free ride" and add a little class to the old rag.

How are many-hued illustrations reproduced with four inks? Look at a printed color reproduction under a magnifying glass. (TIP: The best glass for general editorial voyeurism is an Agfa Lupe 8-power magnifier, available at most camera and graphics shops.) In, say, a flesh tone, you will see patterns of halftone dots in each color: yellow, blue, red, and black. The dots of each color were printed in a separate run past a press cylinder with that color ink. One color was printed on top of another. When the dots combine in exactly the desired position (**registration**), they form blended colors to the eye. If the dots of one color are printed slightly out of position, or **out of register**, the detail of the color reproduction will look smudged.

Very fine color reproduction may use more than four basic inks—and will cost a pile more for the extra-fine adjustments of the press (**makeready**), the runs through the press, and the ink itself, not to mention the preliminary separation (see below) and platemaking work.

Separation. Here is a term every editor should know, and it has nothing to do with unhappy couples. In preparation for four-color printing, a craftsperson called a **color separator** uses special photographic filtering or electronic color-scanning techniques to extract, from the original art, each component process hue: yellow, blue, red, and black. The result is four sheets of film or four color "seps," which are screened into halftones. The red separation will have an image only where the filtered camera, or scanner, "saw" red in the original, and likewise for each of the other colors. The image, after screening, consists of dot patterns.

So you've got four sheets of film which have cost some $300–$600 to produce. Now what? The films don't even carry color on their own; merely a pattern of dots and an identification label, e.g., "Blue." But at the printer, when each separation is transferred to a metal plate by a photo-etch process, when each metal plate is wrapped around a press cylinder and inked the designated process color, and when each of the four color plates hits a rubber blanket that hits a piece of paper, all in the same area—voilà, the broken-up color of the original is put back together again!

If the process already seems elaborate, take a look at the separation and printing bills to see how many little corrections and refinements color work ordinarily involves. And it's a process in which all the gremlins, all of Murphy's laws, are in ready reserve. When things go wrong, and a flesh tone turns out roughly the color of slag, the printer will inevitably blame the separator; the separator will blame the printer or the original artist; and your readers will blame you. Adding color to your publication is not to be taken lightly; but then, what is that's worth anything?

Matched color. Color achieved simply by instructing the printer to use a specific color ink to match, as closely as possible, a single desired color. No camera or electronic separations are involved. The editor or art director's tool for choosing the ink is a catalog of a manufacturer's standard colors, scores of them, each with a code number. One set of standard ink colors is the **PMS system**. A matched color can be used at full strength (solid) or lightened by use of percentage screens. Two or more matched colors also can be combined on press in a **process** sequence (see above), but only the most sophisticated art directors will use this technique to good advantage.

The most common use of a matched color is as a second color in addition to black, applied to a specific, isolated element of the page: a heading, a decoration, an initial capital, a tint block, a detail of a linecut, or, if a splendid enough color can be found and good taste abandoned, the names of the editors on the masthead.

You are now, in the eyes of those who speak no Offset, a graphics expert. Do not abuse your newly gained power, but use it to work with art-production staff and suppliers to save money, time, and mental health. And above all, to enhance the quality of your product.

10

Basic Photography for Editors

CAMERA OPERATION, PICTURE-TAKING, AND PHOTO EDITING

EDITORS WHO HAVE NEVER ADVANCED beyond snapshot photography usually bring a snapshot mentality to editorial graphics. Unless an art director is watching their every move, they publish unpublishable pictures sent in by authors, choose badly from inadequate stock collections, or depend on the staff artiste who takes stunning feline portraits.

The next step up from snapshot-shooting is thoughtful photography with the standard tool of the photojournalists, the 35-millimeter camera. More on the 35-mm in a moment; but first, a few reasons why I have taught every editor I have supervised enough photography for them to advance this one crucial step:

—The editors gain a better sense of the use of photos in a publication; they begin to think photos, to think good composition, and to reject photojournalism that fails to live up to the criteria established for text. Pictorial standards should never be lower than those for text, especially when one realizes that pictorial communication receives more attention. Whether or not an editor will ever take photos for publication, or even assign them or lay them out, a little camera experience will show up eventually in enhanced editorial creativity.

—The reader gains expanded coverage. When editors who cover events in the field can bring home decent photos as well as literate reports, the reader gets a break—a bigger break if the editor deletes the ten thousand words a good picture is worth. Publications not used to having editor/reporters who can take photos on their routine assignments will be much enlivened by this new graphic dimension.

—Editors in specialized fields take newsier pictures than hack photographers. Hire the usual commercial studio to cover a conference, and you get two hundred photos of people sucking ice cubes or holding up plaques. Staff editors know what distinguishes their specialized events from all others, and they can take the photos that tell stories and complement the prose narrative.

—The rights for expanded or subsequent use of each staff photo are available in-house. On some publications, staffers find they can earn a side income selling their specialized photos elsewhere, especially if their specialty becomes topical in the general media.

—Finally, picture-taking is fun. It livens up the routine assignments and does wonders for staff morale. And from what I have observed of morale on most staffs, I would advise an immediate trip to the camera store.

The crash-training course below is divided into three parts. For the first, how to operate a camera, some equipment in hand would be helpful. The second offers picture-taking wisdom, and the third is a miniguide to photo editing, with glossary.

Part One: Hands-On Basics

Equipment needed to get started:

A. One 35-mm, single-lens reflex (SLR) camera body, with shutter-speed and aperture controls (either manual or automatic/manual) and interchangeable lens mount. Any of the

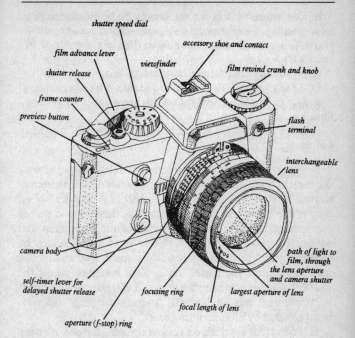

shutter speed dial

film advance lever

shutter release

frame counter

preview button

accessory shoe and contact

viewfinder

film rewind crank and knob

flash terminal

interchangeable lens

camera body

self-timer lever for delayed shutter release

focusing ring

aperture (f-stop) ring

focal length of lens

largest aperture of lens

path of light to film, through the lens aperture and camera shutter

popular, middle-priced brands will do: Canon, Nikon, Pentax, Minolta, Olympus, Yashica, Konica, Vivitar, and so on.* For any given brand, your camera dealer will advise you on the type of equipment available should you wish to enlarge your system.

*Why 35-mm photography instead of instant-type snapshots? Five big reasons: (1) a decent 35-mm camera can provide sharper focus; (2) the interchangeable-lens feature allows for more variety: wide-angle, normal, portrait, telescopic, etc.; (3) a roll of 35-mm film comes with up to 36 exposures, cheap to buy and develop; (4) 35-mm cameras and lenses provide precise controls for the amount and duration of light reaching the film, which means more types of shots are possible and more creativity can be applied to each; (5) 35-mm cameras have many other features—such as delayed-release shutter—to add further dimensions to picture-taking. There are additional reasons to make the switch, some very technical. But take it on faith that snapshots are bush league and rarely suitable for a quality publication. The designation "35-mm," by the way, comes from the width of the film used in all such cameras.

B. One matching lens for the camera body. Recommended focal length: 35-mm (moderately wide-angle); recommended *f*-stop (I'll explain these terms later. Just get the goods in hand.): *f*/2.8.

C. A protective case for the camera-with-lens.

D. A "sky" filter to fit the lens and protect it from scratches.

E. Five or six rolls of fast (ISO 400 or above) black-and-white film.

F. Soft lens paper and blower brush for cleaning off smudges and dust.

Be sure to safeguard the instruction booklets that come with the camera body and lens. These booklets used to be written in strange English: "Please to insert eyeball in viewfinder." Now, with gentle prose and lavish illustrations, they serve as well as any mentor to teach basic operations of the equipment and options for more exotic use.* Follow these booklets step by step, and you'll learn how to hold the camera, load and unload the film, change the lenses, replace the batteries, adjust the controls, and press the shutter release. I will offer just a few tips to supplement this fundamental "camera-handling" information provided by most manufacturers.

1. Never force anything on a camera or lens. If it doesn't work smoothly, you're doing it wrong.

2. You can always remove a lens without exposing the film. Although it does look as if the guts are being dangerously bared with the lens off, the film is exposed only when the shutter or the back of the camera is opened.

3. The most common mechanical problem suffered by beginners is improper loading, so that the film never begins to

---

*If your camera and its instruction booklet have been long parted, look up the manufacturer's address at a library and write for help. Libraries will also have basic photography books, with general instructions for handling 35-mm cameras. Most brands of camera have similar controls. If you learn how to operate one, you can quickly figure out another.

advance to the shutter—even though the photographer is clicking away at the picture of a lifetime. A wretched experience! There is, however, a simple way of checking to see if the film is properly engaged and advancing. Try it the next time you load the camera:

a. With film loaded and back closed, turn the film-advance lever and press the shutter release. Repeat twice.

b. Turn the rewind knob (on the camera's left, with the lens facing away from you) very gently clockwise until you meet a sudden resistance. You are taking up the slack on the spool of film.

c. Turn the film-advance lever again. *If the film is properly engaged, the rewind knob will turn as the lever is advanced.*

4. Practice with black-and-white film, which is relatively cheap. Fire off hundreds of shots to get the feel of the camera. Shoot a dozen pictures of a subject to get one that's decent. Hang the cost. Remember, you can purchase and develop about 500 frames of black-and-white film for less than the price of one photo assigned to a studio professional.

5. When the film-advance lever meets solid resistance before completing its full swing, you're out of film. Whatever frame number the little film-counter window may show, don't force the lever any farther and don't swing open the back of the camera in a rush of enthusiasm. (Every amateur makes this mistake once.) Be sure to rewind the film first, or you'll expose it.

Assuming you have acquired the basic equipment, studied the instruction booklets, and played with the controls until they feel comfortable, it is now time to get serious. The key to serious photography is understanding how to control the amount of light striking the film to achieve a desired effect—or, in camera lingo, how to balance aperture and shutter speed. The topic requires some concentration, but needn't be as formidable as some imagine it.

Are camera and lens in hand? Then here we go.

Aperture (f-stop) and Shutter Speed in a Nutshell

Light comes into a camera through a lens and an open shutter. The shutter is a rigid curtain that moves aside when a button is pushed, allowing light to reach the film. When a certain amount of light strikes the surface of film, it affects the chemistry of that film and creates an image, a picture. Too much light, and the picture is overexposed, washed out. Too little, and it's underexposed, just a murky shadow of a picture. Therefore, an exact amount of light must be admitted into a camera to affect the film's chemistry as desired.

Two major factors govern the amount of light striking the film: the width of the lens opening, and the length of time the shutter is held aside. The size of a lens opening is called its aperture. How long a shutter stays open is referred to as shutter speed.

The aperture openings are measured in f-stops, and it will only be confusing to know what the "f" means right now. It's bad enough that the most common f-stops are the bizarre figures 1.4, 1.8, 2, 2.8, 3.5, 4, 5.6, 6.3, 8, 11, 16, and 22. And that the bigger the number, the smaller the hole it represents! On most commonly used camera lenses, the range is about $f/2$ (large hole) to $f/16$ (small hole).

The shutter speed is usually measured in fractions of a second, one second, and two seconds. So the common range—the length of time the hole stays open automatically when the shutter is tripped—is $1/1,000$ of a second (lightning-fast) to two seconds (slow enough to blur any close movement).

Again, half the mystique of serious photography is in the balance between how wide the hole is open and how long. Since the total amount of light required for a correct exposure is more or less a constant, a wide opening has to be balanced by a quick speed. Or a small opening by a slow speed. How does one know when the two are balanced? On most modern cameras (manual or "manual-mode") a built-in light meter, visible as you focus, points very clearly to a marker when the light is balanced. Above the marker, too much light; below, too little.

But the question arises: Why even think about these two variables—shutter speed and lens opening—when most modern camera systems can automatically calculate and adjust one or the other or both? Here are some examples of the automatic features available:

—With electronic sensing devices, a **shutter-priority** camera will automatically set the correct lens opening to balance whichever shutter speed you select. If you select a speedy 1/1,000 of a second, say, to freeze a hyperactive brat in his tracks, your camera/lens system will measure the light on the subject and automatically set the aperture just wide enough to compensate for the short time the shutter was open. If the available light is inadequate even at the largest aperture, a warning signal will tell you so. You then select a slower shutter speed—perhaps 1/500 —and try it again.

—An **aperture priority** system allows you to choose the lens opening and leave the shutter speed to the camera's electronic brain. Suppose your assignment, you poor devil, is a portrait of Pavarotti with the Paris Opera House in the background. Since you want both tenor and architectural temple in sharp focus, you will choose a small aperture. As will be explained below, the smaller the aperture, the greater the depth of focus. So $f/22$ or $f/16$ is selected manually, and the camera automatically picks a shutter speed for correct light balance.

—Some cameras enable the user to switch from one priority to the other.

—"Instant" cameras, usually with a built-in lens, provide a fixed shutter speed and a light-sensitive device that opens the aperture to the correct f-stop for the available light.

—"Idiot" cameras, as they are snobbishly dubbed, may be of the instant variety or very sophisticated, interchangeable systems. But the shutter and aperture settings will be chosen automatically. Idiot and even professional cameras may also have an "auto-focus" mechanism that figures out the distance to the target object and brings it into focus as sharply as an eagle-eyed old pro could do it manually.

—A new type of camera developed by Sony works on electromagnetic video principles, recording light as digital electronic signals and storing this information on erasable discs. A digital- rather than chemical-based photography opens up new worlds of possible automation. A camera might even be programmed some day to recognize faces in a crowd and zoom in on them. The CIA will love it.

So why bother figuring out shutter speed and aperture or even focusing when electronics can do it all for you? Why not just aim and shoot?

The answer, if you haven't guessed by now, is *fine control*. Automatic cameras balance f-stop with shutter speed to achieve one object only: an exposure that is not overlit or underlit. A photographer balancing the two factors manually, however, can achieve the correct exposure *plus* any number of special objectives: sharp focus throughout the photo, selective focus only, blurred action, stopped action, backlighting, halos and overlighting, shadows and underlighting, and so on.

The exposure for a given subject may be correctly balanced at many combinations of f-stop and shutter speed. For example, $f/2$ at $1/1,000$ may admit the same amount of light as $f/16$ at $1/30$. But the look of the photo may be vastly different for each setting. We can understand why a slow and fast shutter speed would produce different results with a moving object. What difference does size of aperture make?

Depth of Field

Aperture size makes a big difference, thanks to one of the major principles of fine photography: *The smaller the lens opening, the greater the range of sharp focus*.

With a tiny lens opening ($f/22$), just about everything from foreground to infinity will be in focus. A huge opening ($f/1.4$) and only what *you focus on* sharply will be clear—say, everything from 10 to 13 feet away from you. The background will be a blur. You pick the center of focus—foreground, middle ground, or background—by turning the big, textured "focusing ring" of your lens until the object of your desire appears sharp in the viewer. Most viewers have further visible devices to help you focus sharply.

For any given aperture of a camera lens, the area in focus is called **depth of field**. The term seems to have frightened thousands away from serious photography. Perhaps they misheard it as "*death* of field" or shied from a term with a sound of physics to it. But one needs no physics to see what's fuzzy and what's clear for each lens opening. On most cameras, a "preview button" enables you to see the full area that will be in focus when the picture is taken at a given aperture, not just the object you have focused on sharply through the lens. Your camera lens also has a scale marked off on one of its rings to help you estimate the depth of field for each aperture. See your instruction booklet on how to read this scale.

Controlling the depth of field by selecting the right aperture enables you to emphasize figures at any distance from the lens, de-emphasizing other objects in the foreground or background by keeping them out-of-focus. Or, with enough light, it permits sharp focus from arm's reach to infinity. The photographer can pre-select a precise stretch of space before the camera for crisp detail, and blur the rest artfully into a "framing" design. But always, this depth-of-field control through aperture setting must be balanced by a shutter speed that (a) assures enough light, and (b) does not throw the picture off. For example, if light is low and a small aperture calls for a long shutter exposure—say, 1/8 second—the camera cannot be hand-held without all detail blurring. A larger aperture, with less depth of field, may be necessary unless extra lighting can be put on the subject.

An exercise you can try with one of your office colleagues will give you a good idea of depth of field. Imagine he or she—let's say she—has been named editor-in-chief and needs a press photo to go with the happy announcement. Seat her at a desk with a bookshelf or bulletin board in the background. At the front of the desk put a card with her name and new title written on it. Now take your 35-mm camera, 35-mm lens, and a roll of ISO 400 black-and-white film and try to achieve the three effects below (and don't forget, you can control light considerably with office light switches and window blinds):

1. Foreground in soft focus (recognizable but hazy, as if seen through gauze); colleague's face and torso in sharp focus; background items in moderately sharp focus.

2. Foreground in moderately sharp focus; colleague in sharp focus; background in soft focus.

3. Foreground in soft focus; colleague in sharp focus; background in soft focus.

Speed Control

The ability to select your area of focus, of emphasis and de-emphasis, is one advantage of using quality cameras rather than instants. Another is the range of shutter speeds, perhaps easier to comprehend than depth of field. Here's the story: Fast speeds such as 1/1,000 and 1/2,000 capture such a minute period of movement that the action seems frozen—the baseball stuck on the end of a bat; the droplets in a splash of water suspended like jewels. Very slow speeds—say, 1/15 or 1/8 of a second—allow the moving image to slide across the surface of the film and create a blur. Lengthier exposures track an object's gradual movement, such as the path of the moon across the night sky. Intentional blurring can be used to suggest fast motion in an action photo. Experiment with different shutter speeds as well as different depths of focus and, like a painter, you will begin to discover the creative possibilities beyond the strictly representational.

Such creative control is most precise in the "manual" or "match-needle" mode of your camera; but there is much to be said for the electronic, automatic features noted earlier. Photojournalism doesn't often allow for the luxury of fine control; it calls for a fast choice of shutter speed or aperture and reliance on the camera to figure out the rest. The cameras do so fairly well for producing normal, adequately lit exposures. But photographers who understand the manual operations of a camera will also know what the camera's electronic brains are thinking and when those brains are confused. Such photographers will never become the idiots that idiot cameras can make of the less alert.

Processing and Camera Care

Take the film to a local all-purpose lab or your camera store for development. Stay away from drugstore and other discount services. Your order should say: "Develop and contact." In a day or so, you'll get some strips of negative film and an 8 × 10 "contact" sheet with the negatives "proofed" in rows, each frame a miniature black-and-white positive. You'll examine these and choose a few to be blown up as finished photographs.

Develop the film promptly. Keep it away from heat, dust, and strong light. The camera and lenses, too, should be stored in a dark, cool area. All glass surfaces—lenses, mirrors, viewers, etc.—should be protected by their cases and cleaned only with brush and lens paper. Blow and brush away dirt particles, breathe on the lens, and clean it very gently with the paper. Don't rub scratches into it.

Part Two: Better Pictures

While learning the mechanics of shooting, worry mainly about sharp focus and adequate light exposure. Start thinking about picture content only when the camera begins to feel less like a live grenade in your hands and more like a creative instrument. Thousands of texts are available for the high achiever on the subject of artful photography, from the "tips-for-better-picture-taking" pamphlets put out by photographic firms to the magnificent *Life Library of Photography*. But for the editor who simply wants to be steered in the right direction, right now, here are a few guidelines—the golden rules, most will agree—of general photojournalism. The rules apply as well to photo-editing—choosing, cropping, and arranging photos for publication—for in a sense the first editing is being done in the camera. (More on this in Part Three.)

1. *Take at least four or five shots to get one.*

You see the pros doing it, "blow-up" style, shooting as fast as they or an automatic power winder can advance the film. It is not only stylish, it's essential. There are twenty or thirty variables in most journalistic picture situations, everything from the subject blinking to people entering the background. Getting all these variables to behave themselves in a single shot is like winning the sweepstakes. Shoot steady, squeezing the shutter release rather than punching it to avoid camera shake; but shoot fast, before your subject loses patience and the scene changes altogether. When *you* create a variation, such as turning the camera for a vertical shot (see below), asking the subject to change expression, or shifting your angle, take still another four or five. The pros take hundreds in a session, including many "bracketed" shots (normal *f*-stop, one *f*-stop below normal, and one *f*-stop above).

2. *Think horizontal* and *vertical.*

I have done everything but karate-kick beginning photographers to get them to turn the camera every so often into the vertical-frame position. Unlike most instant cameras, the 35-mm SLR yields a non-square, rectangular picture. If the subject is basically horizontal, shoot it in the normal (horizontal) position. If it is tall or otherwise suggestive of verticality, turn that camera! Turn it so that the long sides of the rectangle are straight up and down.

3. *Get close enough to fill the frame with the* real *subject.*

The mark of amateur photography is the distant subject, lost in a vast and irrelevant background. Amateurs are not satisfied with their mates posed at the door to an old cathedral. They must back up until mate, spires, and Heaven itself are included in the picture. Don't retreat from your photos. Move in on that face or detail you want to show, and leave the panoramic backgrounds to the postcard photographers.

The key to journalistic and general artistic impact is *selectivity*—not comprehensiveness. Select the detail that explodes with meaning; eliminate the parts that simply lie there as clutter or background. Yes, you might lose something in the way of setting; but you gain sharper concentration on an object *you* have chosen uniquely for photographic interpretation.

If the setting truly enhances your subject, then take the overall shot (sometimes called the "establishing" shot). But, on pain of death, do not fail to capture the telling detail as well before it escapes your camera forever. The basic 35-mm lens I have recommended will allow for good close-ups of any subject that can be approached physically. Later, driven by your reluctance to approach a rabid baboon, you will want to acquire telephoto and other special-effect lenses for your close-ups.

"Zoom" lenses, which in motion pictures produce godlike swoops from long shots to close-ups, are available for still cameras and very seductive in concept. Here, after all, is a lens that can be lengthened from "normal" to telephoto without removing it from the camera. In practice, however, most beginners are disappointed with the average zoom lens. It is heavy and bulky, very difficult to hold steady, and—excluding those costing the earth—requires bright light for a decent picture. I would not recommend one for beginners or for the average requirements of photojournalism.

4. *Eliminate clutter*.

Moving in close eliminates most distracting clutter from the composition, but not all. The careful photographer scans the foreground as well as the background for bright or obtrusive objects that will draw the eye away from the subject; objects which seem to be growing out of the subject's head or which otherwise disrupt the photo's key outlines; faces or bodies other than the subject's, especially those threatening to steal the show or belie the theme (e.g., loneliness) of the photograph; and elements that cheapen the aesthetic effect or date an otherwise timeless theme. A parked car is such an element, as destructive to photographic as to environmental atmosphere.

Clutter may be removed physically, by changing the angle of the shot, or by focusing-out: selecting a shallow depth of field.

5. *Avoid harsh lighting.*

Stark light from one source may be desirable for certain architectural representations or theatrical effects; but most often lighting must be softened or balanced for good pictures. The worst lighting situations are: midday sun, under which details are either blindingly overexposed or lost in shadow and in which the human face takes on the features of a giant panda; overhead incandescent (nonfluorescent) bulbs, the light from which spills like thick yogurt on the pates, noses, and shoulders of the subjects below; and flash illumination, which turns any object between subject and camera into a blazing mass of white and leaves the background as dreary as a parking lot closed for the night.

The antidotes are many and don't always require expensive lighting equipment. Among the simplest are these: To avoid midday sun, find some nice even shade, or shoot soon after dawn or in late afternoon. Flash illumination (not addressed in this chapter) can be used to fill in shadows in bright outdoor light. To avoid the spilt-yogurt look of overhead incandescent lighting, move the subjects outdoors or to more favorable indoor light: a room bright with fluorescent lighting and, ideally, some window light. Always keep the light sources out of the picture unless going for a special effect, such as a silhouette against the window. A second means of avoiding a spilt-yogurt effect is to have the subject look up until more light falls on the face—but the subject should not seem to be gargling. A third way is to overexpose the picture slightly: Change the aperture or shutter speed until the meter falls solidly into the "plus" area; some facial detail, though possibly grainy, will emerge. A fourth method is to reflect some light back up toward the face.

A white tablecloth or the pages of a large open book might help if they are appropriate to the picture or can be cropped out.

Flash-illuminated photos, in my opinion, are always ugly. They are least ugly when the foreground is clear and the subject is at the exact distance recommended for the flash device. It may also help to use flash units that can be aimed other than head-on at the subject. Flash as supplementary fill-in light is probably the most aesthetic.

Although I finally gave in, I worked without flash for ten years, publishing hundreds of photos in national magazines and rarely being the worse off on an assignment. Learn to shoot in available light without flash (using the remarkable light-sensitive films with speeds up to ISO 2500); then advance to flash with the help of your camera dealer and manufacturer's instructions.

6. *Shoot fronts, not backs.*

It sounds like a simple rule, yet an astonishing number of photos are taken, and even published, with no greater theme than the backs of people's heads. Now and then the problem may be circumstantial, but more often the fault lies with the photographer's shyness. If the subject is an audience, get in *front* of it and show faces. You may feel hideously conspicuous, but the crowd perceives you as no more than the usual paraphernalia surrounding a public event.

In photographing athletes and other performers, be sure to hustle your way into head-on views. Action coming at the camera is almost always more interesting than action going away. (But for variety and other aesthetic considerations, break this and all other rules from time to time. Nat Fein's "Babe Ruth Strikes Out" shows a back view of big Number 3, with head bowed, during farewell ceremonies for the Babe in 1948. A front view might have lost the mood.)

7. *Consider the subject-eye-level shot.*

Amateurs aim down at small children and animals, diminishing them to insignificance. Better photographers usually try a few shots from the eye-level of the subject or even shoot up at it from the ground. Tall objects, too, may have more impact when shot eye-to-eye from a high vantage point. Vary the vertical angles of your shots, and move *around* the subjects as well, exploring side views.

8. *Build a third dimension of depth.*

A photo is not a sculpture, and sometimes two-dimensionality should be emphasized. For example, the flattening effect of long lenses (85-mm and above) is used to create such popular shots as a harbor full of sailboats, all seemingly the same distance from the camera in a fabriclike pattern of triangles. But flatness can also rob many a photograph of its potential drama, texture, and action. Depth can add these qualities.

To dramatize the length of a line waiting to see a new Woody Allen movie release, a photographer might lean over a roof and try to show it all. But a safer and more interesting shot might be from the head of the line looking back toward the end, showing as many faces as possible. The choice of lens is determined by two desired effects: (a) a great depth of field, so that the first and last faces are in focus; and (b) an exaggerated illusion of depth, so that a block-long line seems to snake away for miles. Only the wide-angle lenses—35-mm and below—satisfy both demands.

The general techniques for creating a feeling of depth with wide-angle lenses are (a) to get close to the nearest subject, and (b) to look for at least one element that continues from foreground to background. With the movie line, it might be the sidewalk, so get down low and include it in the composition from near to far.

Even the most prosaic group portraits can be enlivened by adding depth. Instead of four family members up against the aluminum siding, why not use sky as background and stagger their distances from the camera by a few feet, making sure that one does not obscure another and that all are within the range of focus? The effect can be overdone, especially with executives spread all over an office like circus acrobats; but more often depth is not even considered, much to the photographer's disadvantage.

9. *Use frames of reference and framing elements.*

One of the most common tools of composition is the framing element, a subordinate shape that surrounds the main subject or somehow sets it off and gives it scale. Window frames, wrought-iron gates, and stone arches are some of the common elements used to frame country scenes; cityscapes might be framed by tall bridges, modern sculptures, old lampposts, and so on. These, along with palm trees and wagonwheels, are the clichés; but good photographers will always look for shapes that will help define the size and placement of the subject. Often the framing element is in the foreground, but subdued by silhouetting or soft focus. Such foreground, which should be interesting but not overwhelming, also adds depth—a third dimension that pulls the viewer into the photo.

10. *Take office shots out of the office.*

Photographs of people in offices, even of executives, can usually be improved by shooting them elsewhere than in the office environment, which was never designed for portraits. Offices are either too cluttered or too sterile, unevenly lit, too small for good photographic maneuvering, or simply too much like every other office to give the photo any distinction. Go outside. Find an old wall or a tree trunk as background. Away from the main source of stress, the subject will loosen up.

If the assignment does call for an interior office shot, be imaginative but not bizarre. Climb on a chair to get a downward angle, but not on a ladder for an aerial view. An executive might be asked to sit on the edge of the desk, but not Buddha-style on its center. And remember: Keep the window light behind or well to the side of the camera.

11. *Reveal the character.*

How to pose the subject? Although portrait photography is beyond the scope of this chapter, a few general tips might be helpful. A good pose ought to suggest the character of the subject, not exaggerate it. Use body language: folded arms, tilts of the head, chin lowered or raised. Hands touching the cheeks or supporting the chin add an element of sensitivity—verging on silliness. If a character is most natural in a deep frown, don't force a smile. Imagine Winston Churchill with a big, toothy grin. Half smiles or closed-lip smiles lend mystery. The degree to which eyes face the camera will also affect character. Use these variables until the composite picture adds up to a personality. Shoot three or four of each pose to avoid catching a blinking eyelid at halfmast.

12. *Premeditate.*

"The captured moment"—that fleeting instant when a truth is revealed—is what all photographers seek. What most of them get instead is a cliché: a situation so common as to leave the viewer reeling under a double dose of déjà vu. Let's face it; even at its most romantic, life is a visual cliché: the stallion galloping along the beach, the couple against the sunset, the young mother at the lace curtains. And business life is even duller visually than it is intellectually.

What is the photographer to do with the moment that isn't worth capturing, that simply lies there?

Whenever time allows, the good photographer premeditates. The subject is set up in the mind's eye, moved about, angled, segmented, shown in all its variety. If the assignment is a portrait, the photographer makes rough sketches of possible poses, cases out the setting and available props, plans for additional settings, and plots the lighting.

The photojournalist thinks ahead to the layout. Should most photos be vertical or horizontal? Would a sequential series of about six shots work well across two pages? Are there enough quotations for several mug shots? Will there be space on the pages for long shots, medium shots, and close-ups of minute details?

Layouts that capture a moment of life unfolding, that leap off the page, are usually no accident; they are planned well before the shooting.

Part Three: Photo Editing

I can hardly make you into a crack photo editor in a few pages; but if the preceding guidelines have improved your picture-taking concepts, you are already ahead of many editors who think their natural sense of design and a pile of stock prints will dress up any page. Photo-editing, after all, is mainly an extension of photographic skills. Most of the dozen pointers I've just discussed can be applied to what photo editors do.

Depending on the type of publication, photo editors may be those responsible for everything to do with photos, from assignment to layout; they may be the art directors, who handle photos along with other types of illustrations; or they may be staff editors who take a turn at choosing, cropping, sizing, and laying out the photos for their departments.

The beginning staffer is likely to fall into this last category in many editorial offices. I did—first as a public information assistant and later as an associate magazine editor. I'd like to pass along just a few definitions* that would have helped me at the outset, and then some brief comments on applying the principles of picture-taking to photo-editing.

Some terms-with-tips

Frame. Each picture on a roll of film. The frames are identified by numbers on the developed rolls.

Contact sheet. Positive proofs of all the frames on a roll of developed film, the same size as on the film (35-mm wide for 35-mm cameras). The proofs are not in perfect focus and do not show all the tones that can be achieved when each frame is processed into a print. But the editor, working with a magnifying viewer, can pick out the most promising frames for enlargement. Proof sheets larger than contact size can also be ordered.

*Chapter 9 offers further definitions related to processing photos for publication.

Transparency. You know it as a slide. Four-by-five and 8 × 10-inch transparencies are also common. Color transparencies can be converted into black-and-white negatives and prints. Only color transparencies (translucent) can be reproduced for color publication, never color prints (opaque).

Cropping. From a full photo, selecting the area to be reproduced and indicating it on a tissue overlay or with **crop marks** on the margins of the original print. Were they to be extended across the photo, the vertical and horizontal crop marks would intersect and define the rectangle to be reproduced. The picture editor can consider various rectangular areas within one photo by framing each with a pair of L-shaped pieces of cardboard. Other geometric shapes, such as circles, may also be cropped out of a photo.

Outlining. A staff artist or the photoengraver can outline an object in a photo so that it reproduces without any background—standing out on the white of the page. Objects with simple edges—like a ball or bald head—will give outliners fewer ulcers than harps, trees, and heads of curly hair.

Enlargement or **blowup**. A picture reproduced larger than the original print.

Reduction. Reproduced smaller than the original.

Bleed. A picture extending all the way to one or more edges of a trimmed page. Before trimming, the picture extends to the **bleed edge** of the page, which is about one-eighth inch beyond where the page will be cut. Bleed photos, then, must have "enough picture" to reach the bleed edge. This extra margin allows for an inadequate trim, which would leave a thin white edge otherwise.

An **inside bleed** extends into the center gutter, where no trim margin is necessary. Bleeds filling up one page or more of a two-page spread are very special, and should be reserved for high quality photos meriting extraordinary attention.

Sizing, or **scaling,** for reproduction. Finding the ratio between the original dimensions of a piece of art and the proportional dimensions of the desired reproduction. The result is a precise reduction or enlargement ratio called **focus,** which is passed along to the photoengraver with the art. Focus (symbolized by F) is expressed as a percentage of the original. If the photo of a chocolate bar is to be enlarged to a mouthwatering three times its original size, F equals 300 percent. If a picture of a diseased tooth is to be reduced, mercifully, to one third its original dimensions, F equals 33-½ percent (percentages are usually rounded to the nearest half).

The technique of scaling is learned on the job if not in art school, and there are as many techniques as there are ways to figure out missing quantities in a proportional equation $a/b = c/d$. The fastest way, however, is with a calculator. Unfortunately, many editors are still sizing with a device called a "scaling wheel," which is slow, hard to read, and can slip and cause errors. On a calculator, sizing is a matter of finding proportions by lightning-fast division and multiplication: If the width of the original is 63 and must become 14 to fit a column, the ratio is 14/63 or 14 divided by 63, or—bing, bing on the calculator—22 percent; and the other dimensions are proportional. It gets more complicated, but can be figured out from a basic formula: $F = R/O$. Focus percentage equals Reproduction dimension divided by the corresponding Original dimension. The necessary variations of the formula are $R = F \times O$, and $O = R \div F$.

Give the calculator method a try, but use any method that works efficiently for you. As with most editorial matters, the result is what counts; the importance of technique can be blown out of all—well, proportion.

Now let's look back on those dozen elements for good picture-taking (see pp. 132–138). The first advised taking four or five shots to get one. The photo editor *studies* those four or five (or more) before choosing one for a layout. Photo editors must see as many variations on a theme as possible to select those that will sweetly complement a text. Photographers like to show only their best prints off a roll. Editors should insist on seeing the full proof sheet, for they may find special virtues in one of the photographer's rejects. Like photographers, editors favor shots containing some action, beauty, emotion, and information; but editors also look for light-and-shadow characteristics that will hold up throughout the photoengraving and printing processes. Dark, moody scenes that would hang very well in a gallery might look like specimens of volcanic ash by the time they are printed on coarse stock. Only those editors working with art-quality printers and deluxe coated papers can hope to reproduce all the delicate gradations of a black-and-white photo or the juicy, translucent hues of an original color transparency.

The second "golden rule" for picture-taking was to shoot horizontals and verticals of each subject. The photo editor now takes advantage of the variations by thinking depth as well as width in the layouts. Editors are always on the watch for shots that can be laid out radically tall or wide—a train crossing six columns; a basketball giant slam-dunking two points within the top margin. The editors also look for varied shapes within the photographer's original rectangle, sometimes cropping a vertical out of a horizontal or vice versa.

Just as the photographer tries to fill the frame with the subject and eliminate clutter (points 3 and 4), so the editor usually crops in all the way to the object of interest unless the background conveys indispensable information. Often the object of interest is only a small area cropped from the original photo and has to be enlarged to fit a layout. How much a photo can be enlarged without deteriorating into a grainy blur depends on sharpness of focus and the type of film the photographer used. Generally, the more light-sensitive the film, the grainier. It's best to start with a big, sharp photo when you're trying a radically tight crop—say, down to someone's mouth.

Enlarging a small detail involves the risk of losing sharp focus. Reducing large areas to fit small spaces has its own hazards. For every photo there is a minimum point of "message delivery." A glorious mountain range will no longer look glorious when it is squeezed into one column. Eyes still devastating at an 80-percent reduction (80 percent of the original photo) become flyspecks at 20 percent. One of the most persistent follies of amateur picture editors is squeezing five or six decent photos into a page layout when the best two or three would have had far more impact.

Each photo has to be judged independently for how far it can be reduced, but very few 8×10 pictures can go below 30 percent and still be worth 10,000 words. Editors—especially those who have taken the pictures—hate to leave any good shots on the layout table; but perhaps the most valuable single piece of advice I can pass along in this section is this: Select one-third of the photos you were going to run, and run them three times the size.

From picture-taking pointers 5 through 12, you can extrapolate well enough on your own when the time comes to work with photographs on the page or with photographers. Scores of texts treat the finer points of photo layout, telling us never to crop off fingers, bleed noses into margins, or fear to stretch a leg across the gutters. But since mine is a friendly guide, I want mainly to get you started on the pleasures of good photography, which will lead you willingly to the rest.

Afterword:
The Electronic Editor

When electronic editing installations were still rare, *Crain's Chicago Business* had the audacity to set up a fancy system just a block away from my tradition-bound editorial offices. Moreover, it did so in a street-level, glass-walled newsroom whose occupants could be seen shamelessly interacting with their video display terminals. I had to see it each morning on my way to work; I had to feel the gaze of those green-eyed cathode ray tubes, mocking my attachment to typewriters and blue pencils.

I vowed I would not be intimidated. We were doing just fine with our manual systems. But as each day passed and the green eyes hypnotized me, it began to seem we were not doing so well at all. I realized I would not rest until I saw the electronic operation close up, and I arranged for a visit.

To my amusement, the system was down when I arrived. But before I could say, "Har, har—so much for progress!" the text popped back on the screens and the editors began scrolling away. My host explained the system briefly, and I asked questions.

When I returned to my office an hour later, it was like entering a medieval scriptorium. I knew at once that I was sold.

My sixty-minute conversion from skeptic to believer was not unusual. Almost without exception, editors who work with video display terminal (VDT) systems testify they are easy to master, remarkable in the range of editorial dirty work they can handle, and beneficial to the editor's creativity. *Folio* magazine listed these main advantages of electronic editing after interviewing editors at five wired-up journals: "It decreases work steps, which decreases the possibility of errors; it allows editors to receive information from outside sources; it can store and organize large amounts of research; it can help promote productivity during writing; and it can be used for management functions." And that was in 1980, when the systems were relatively young.

Not only editors, but writers—from staff reporters to literary lions—have fallen in love with word-processing microcomputers. They welcome the end of messy, revised, cut-and-pasted drafts. They prefer hard-copy printouts on command to typing and retyping till their fingers cramp.

Electronic VDT copy is always clean because the revisions displace (overstrike) the original text, and what isn't overstruck can be instantly deleted. Writers and editors say this orderly environment enables them to think more clearly about content. On many systems, notes and rough drafts can be stored and called up at will, sometimes displayed with the revised draft on a split screen. Blocks of type can be rearranged with ease. Everything is counted and measured automatically. There is little to do, really, but *edit*.

Managers adore the systems because the writers and editors are capturing keystrokes that can be run through other programs, such as typesetting or indexing, or processed into interim information products, all without the costly redundancies of traditional methods, all at lightning speed.

Some people in editing are still apprehensive about the electronic takeover. Seasoned editors without training or work experience in VDTs worry that they are becoming obsolete, especially when they see the many cruel ads insisting on such experience. They need to do what they can to catch up, but it isn't easy to find hands-on training opportunities.

Some worry about how easily the entire editorial function could be bypassed should computer-to-computer communications supplant traditional publishing. From a terminal in the home, office, or laboratory, an author can send text through a switching center to an end user selecting material from a receiving terminal. Will anyone need a middle person called "editor" to process and package the text?

That will depend, says publishing executive Elwood Gannett, on "which we are to save—keystrokes or coherence."* Already there is a thin line, he notes, between informal computer conferencing and on-line "electronic journals." He fears that, at worst, such journals will be unrefereed, unedited, "subject to information pollution," and downright incoherent. The role of the editor—to select, organize, correct, and enhance—will be devalued in favor of speed and cost-cutting.

The apprehensions of Gannett and others are close to being borne out in the sci-tech community, where "compuscripts" of machine-readable articles are submitted by authors to journal editors. Although the editors are still editing, sometimes from an accompanying hard copy, someone is surely weighing how much quality would be lost and how much time gained if the compuscripts went directly to computer typesetting—or were disseminated directly to the author's on-line colleagues.

Editors, no doubt, will have to demonstrate time and again what their work is worth. Not only in electronic journalism, but in book publishing, now threatened by the proliferation of home computers-with-printers. Why should an author not be-

---

*Gannett, director of publishing services for the Institute of Electrical and Electronic Engineers, Inc., offered these observations at a 1981 seminar of the Society of National Association Publications in New York City.

come a cottage publisher, bypassing the editorial services of established publishing houses and distributing raw digital text and printouts directly to a small market at a modest profit?

We must ponder what human editors can do best for authors and readers in the computer age. For computers have learned not only to store, find, sort, and deliver text, but to enhance it. In 1981 Bell Laboratories made news with its Writer's Workbench editing system, a set of integrated programs that can analyze an author's text against rules of American usage. The rules, laboriously synthesized from authoritative language guides and stored in the system's memory, enable the computer to identify passive voice, complex sentences, jargon, clichés, and general wordiness, and to offer helpful suggestions for a rewrite. The system can also correct spelling and some punctuation and grammar.

It could not, in 1981, analyze the organization and logic of a piece of writing, its factual accuracy, insights, symbolic connections, intuitive leaps, tastes, judgments, or impact on an intended audience. It could not brainstorm new projects, break an author's writing block, or spot a libel. Nor could it rewrite.

But someday soon a computer will write straightforward reports and articles. And it will edit itself after a fashion or send the text to another computer for editing, or "massaging," as it is called. And the text will go forth into a delivery system for retrieval by anyone who wants to dial it up. Such text will have its uses, especially in communicating technical data. But there will be limits. Even in the hard sciences and technologies, readers get tired of information overload. Quality drives out quantity. Readers will seek a level of selectivity, clarity, embellishment, and warmth that brain cells seem better able to achieve than microprocessors.

In the computer age we will need editors to write programs for editing systems, and, as usual, editors to make human communications bearable for humans. Editors will help develop new communications formats to supplement the old. Old formats will change in function. The elements of editing will change accordingly.

As for editors, we'll be essentially the same compulsive, underpaid people who exist to keep authors, publishers, and readers in harmony; and if a computer wants to put on a green visor and help us out, it is more than welcome.

Index

Index

Other acclaimed Macmillan classics that will improve your writing skills are available at your local bookstore or by mail. To order directly, return the coupon below to: Macmillan Publishing Company, Special Sales Department, 866 Third Avenue, New York NY 10022.

Line Sequence	ISBN	Author/Title	Price	Quantity
1	0024182001	Strunk & White/ELEMENTS OF STYLE, paper	$3.50	——
2	0024182300	Strunk & White/ELEMENTS OF STYLE, cloth	7.95	——
3	0020474105	Plotnik/THE ELEMENTS OF EDITING, paper	4.95	——
4	0025977008	Plotnik/THE ELEMENTS OF EDITING, cloth	9.50	——
5	0020153805	Roddick/WRITING THAT MEANS BUSINESS, paper	8.95	——
6	0026044005	Roddick/WRITING THAT MEANS BUSINESS, cloth	10.95	——
7	0020475707	Flesch/THE ART OF READABLE WRITING, paper	3.95	——
8	0020463804	Flesch/THE ART OF PLAIN TALK, paper	3.95	——
9	0020154402	Shertzer/THE ELEMENTS OF GRAMMAR, paper	4.95	——

Sub-total ——

Please add postage and handling costs—$1.00 for the first book and 50¢ for each additional book ——

Sales tax—if applicable ——

TOTAL ==

	Lines	Units
Ord. Type REG		

—— Enclosed is my check/money order payable to Macmillan Publishing Company.

—— Bill my —— MasterCard —— Visa Card # _____ Control No. _____   For charge orders only:

Expiration date _____ Signature _____

Charge orders valid only with signature

Ship to: _____   Bill to: _____

_____ Zip Code _____   _____ Zip Code

For information regarding bulk purchases, please write to Special Sales Director at the above address. Publisher's prices are subject to change without notice. Allow 3 weeks for delivery.

FC #278